CONTENTS

MADE IN BRITAIN

Queen Victoria came to the throne in 1837, at the age of eighteen, and reigned over Great Britain until her death in 1901. During her life, enormous changes took place, the most dramatic of which was Britain's transformation from a farming country into a rich industrial nation. When Victoria was born there were about 14 million people in England, Scotland and Wales. Most of these lived and worked in the countryside. By the time the Queen died, this population had risen to over 37 million, most of whom lived in or near rapidly expanding cities and towns, and worked in factories, offices and shops.

▲ *This photograph shows the inside of a Victorian bicycle factory. Photography was invented in the 1820s and 30s, but the cheap portable kodak box camera didn't appear until 1888.*

In Victorian times Great Britain included all of Ireland as well as Scotland, England and Wales.

FULL STEAM AHEAD

Britain's growth as a great industrial and manufacturing nation was largely due to the improvement of the steam engine in the 1780s. Before steam engines were invented, machines could only be powered by wind, water, people or horses. Machines driven by steam were not only more reliable, they were quicker too. Not surprisingly, smart businessmen soon realised that by using steam-powered machinery they could produce goods more cheaply than ever before. So they built factories to house the monstrous new machines and employed lots of people to work in them.

◀ 'Iron and Coal' by W. Bell Scott. The Victorians used steam to power trains and ships as well as furnaces and factory machinery. How many uses for steam can you see in this picture?

Some Victorian farmers bought steam-powered machines to help them produce the extra food needed to feed Britain's growing population. These machines meant that fewer workers were needed, so many farm hands moved to the cities and towns that were springing up around factories to find work.

ON THE RAILS

When Victoria was a child, few people travelled far from home. Those that did usually set off on foot or horseback, or rode along rutted roads in a horse-drawn coach. During the 1800s, however, all this changed. On 27 September 1825, crowds of people lined the 14-kilometre railway track that had been built between the towns of Stockton and Darlington to watch the first ever passenger steam train puff into view. Five years later, the world's first 'inter city' route was opened between Liverpool and Manchester, and by the turn of the century, Britain was covered with over 29,000 kilometres of railway track.

'SPUTTERING NOISY MONSTERS'

Many people dreaded the coming of the railway. Some thought that the 'hammering and roaring and hissing' of the steam trains would lead to milkless cows and eggless hens. Others thought that the engine sparks would set fire to crops. Yet, in spite of these objections, gangs of men called navvies were ordered to dig and blast their way across the countryside, leaving a criss-cross of tunnels, embankments and bridges behind them.

The arrival of the railways had a huge impact on the lives of everyone in Britain. Towns sprang up around the places where trains were built; industrial cities grew even bigger as soon as there was a railway to carry their factory-made goods; and ports too far away from the tracks simply dwindled and died.

▲ The Victorians loved over-the-top decoration. St Pancras Station in London, opened in 1868, looks more like a great church than a railway station.

Speedy train travel also meant that large amounts of fresh foods could be sent long distances without going rotten. And news, that had once taken days to get from town to country, could arrive in a matter of hours.

▲ *Railway companies offered cheap fares to the seaside. This meant that even the poor could afford to hop onto a train and enjoy an afternoon out by the sea.*

ALL ABOARD

In the early days of railways, no one paid much attention to passenger comfort. First class carriages had seats, a roof and covered sides, but second and third class carriages were more like open cattle trucks. Unlike second class passengers, those travelling third class had nothing to sit on. Instead they had to hang on tightly to a handrail to stop themselves tumbling over the sides. No wonder railway company reports were full of references to passenger accidents!

LET YOUR BRAIN TAKE THE STRAIN

The distance between London and York by train is 303 kilometres. In 1840 the journey took 11 hours. The train travelled at an average speed of approximately 27.5 kilometres per hour.

In 1893 the journey took $3^3/4$ hours, at an average speed of about 81 kilometres per hour.

In 1993 the journey took 2 hours.

a. What was the average speed of the 1993 train?
b. In the 2 hours the journey took in 1993, roughly how far would passengers in 1840 have travelled? (Answers on page 30)

The introduction of steam-powered machines and the building of the railways created a great demand for iron, steel and coal. Iron and steel were needed to build machinery and railway tracks. Coal was needed to smelt the iron and steel and to provide fuel for steam engines.

TRAMS AND TRANSPORT

STEAM AND SAILS
The first successful steamships were built in the early 1800s, and by the late 1830s they were steaming their way across the Atlantic Ocean. Although the early steamers had sails, they didn't have to rely on winds. This made them quicker and more reliable than the sailing ships of old, and so helped to bring the most far-off lands within reach of Britain.

Electric trams ran on rails in the street and were powered by overhead cables. Introduced in the 1890s, they soon put horse-drawn omnibuses out of a job.

HORSE POWER
Wealthy Victorians without their own carriages often hired horse-drawn taxis called hansom cabs or growlers. The first buses, called omnibuses, appeared in London in 1829. Pulled by horses, with seats both inside and on the roof, omnibuses were cheaper than cabs, but still too expensive for the poor.

8

ON YER BIKE!

By the end of Victoria's reign, electric trams were adding to the chaos on city roads; electric underground trains were speeding about beneath London's streets; and low-framed safety bicycles were being ridden all over the country. During the late 1880s, cycling became all the rage as bicycles with equal-sized wheels and air-filled tyres were introduced. Two-seater bicycles, called tandems, were popular too, as this Victorian song suggests.

Daisy, Daisy, give me your answer true.
I'm half crazy, all for the love of you!
It won't be a stylish marriage,
I can't afford a carriage,
But you'll look sweet
Upon the seat
Of a bicycle made for two!

This tandem bicycle dates from the 1880s. ▼

The modern motor car was invented in the late 1800s. The first cars in Britain were not allowed to go faster than 6.5 kilometres per hour and each car had to have someone walking ahead of it, to warn others of its approach.

BRIGHT IDEAS

Although the ancient Greeks knew about electrical forces, it wasn't until the Victorian age that electricity was used for lighting, communication and power. Electric street lighting first appeared in London in 1878, and by 1931 about half the homes in England had their own electricity supply. (Victorian homes without electricity were lit by oil or gas lamps and candles).

By the time Victoria died, electricity was also being used to send messages by telephone. Telephones were not a huge success at first because they were expensive, and many people were shy of using them. Wealthy Victorians left their servants to answer the telephone, to save themselves the embarrassment!

9

THE BRITISH EMPIRE

When Victoria came to the throne in 1837, Britain already controlled a mighty empire which included parts of India and Canada and all of Australia. By 1901, this empire included the rest of India, most of Canada and parts of Africa and the Far East as well. These countries were known as the colonies. They provided the Victorians with tea, sugar and other foods which cannot be grown in Britain. They also supplied raw materials like wool and cotton which British factories made into goods. These goods were then sold to other parts of the empire for a huge profit. Without these trading links, Victorian Britain wouldn't have become nearly as wealthy or powerful as it did.

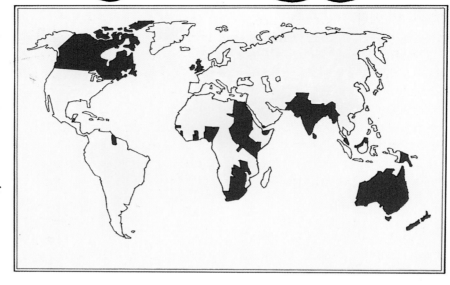

The British Empire in 1901. Britain won control of most of her colonies by fighting for them.

THE BRITISH ABROAD

Hundreds of British people were sent to the colonies to govern them. Many more moved voluntarily to Australia, Canada and New Zealand because they wanted a better life for themselves, away from Britain's overcrowded cities. After the failure of Ireland's potato crop in the 1840s, nearly a million Irish people moved to America to escape starvation.

Like their countrymen back home, the Victorians who lived in the colonies were convinced that 'Britain Was Best'. As a result, they refused to fit in with the local way of life and often behaved as though they had never left Britain.

This picture, which was painted in the early 1850s, shows a group of Victorians on their way to Australia. Can you spot where the couple at the front of the picture are sheltering their baby?

A MODEL QUEEN

When Victoria became Queen, the monarchy was in a bad way. The previous king, William IV, had made himself unpopular by meddling in political affairs. And the king before him, George IV, had been a rotten husband, a greedy eater and a drunk. According to one eyewitness, George IV ate so much that when he undid his corset his belly flopped down to his knees!

By contrast, Victoria was a saint! She neither interfered too much in politics, nor behaved badly. Instead she and her husband, Albert, worked hard, lived simply and spent much of their spare time with their nine children. After the scandalous goings-on of previous monarchs, Victoria and Albert's devotion to each other was a welcome change, and their example of family life was one which many Victorians tried to follow.

SPILLS AND THRILLS

As a young woman, Victoria often spent her evenings playing spillikins with her Prime Minister, Lord Melbourne. To play your own version of spillikins . . .

You will need: a small matchbox full of *used* matches or a packet of cocktail sticks ● a piece of paper with a circle, measuring 10 cm across, drawn on it ● 2 or more players

Spillikins or spellicans became popular in the mid-1800s when sets were often made from bone or ivory in the shape of tools and weapons.

▲Victoria and Albert made the royal family popular. Their mixture of ordinariness and wealth made it easy for prosperous Victorians to identify with them and respect them.

In 1861 Albert died of typhoid fever. In memory of her husband, Victoria had a bridge, a memorial and a round hall built in London, all of which are called . . . Albert. ▶

THE RULES OF THE GAME

Each player takes a match and the rest are scattered inside the circle.

The first player then tries to pull a match out of the circle using his/her matchstick or fingers. If another match is moved by mistake, the first player stops and the next player has a go. If the first player removes a match from the circle without disturbing any of the other matches, he/she has another go.

The winner is the player with the most matches at the end of the game.

LIFE UPSTAIRS

Victorian society was divided into three social groups or classes.

UPPER CLASS

Upper class families were immensely rich and powerful. Many of them owned thousands of acres of land each, which they rented out for a profit, and had a house in town as well as one in the country. Most upper class parents didn't have to work. Their homes and land were looked after by servants, their food was prepared by cooks, and their children were cared for by nannies and taught by governesses. In fact, some young children spent so much time with their nannies and governesses that they knew them better than their own parents.

MIDDLE CLASS

The middle class was made up of a wide range of people, from wealthy bankers, lawyers, factory owners and doctors to less wealthy shopkeepers, clerks and school teachers. All middle class men had to work to support their families, but unlike the working class below them, they never did physical work, such as laying railway lines or working in factories.

▲ *Children from wealthy families spent a lot of time in their nurseries.*

Many middle class Victorian families lived in houses still used today. ▶

KEEPING UP APPEARANCES

The middle class adored the royal family and longed to be considered 'respectable' like their Queen. They dressed smartly every day, kept their homes neat and tidy, and made sure that they did nothing that would shock their neighbours. Many of them also spent hours reading improving books which told them the correct way to do everything, including how to eat cheese!

'When eating cheese, small morsels (pieces) of cheese should be placed with a knife on small morsels of bread, and the two conveyed (carried) to the mouth with thumb and finger, the piece of bread being the morsel to hold as the cheese should not be taken up with the fingers, and should not be eaten off the point of the knife. As a matter of course, young ladies do not eat cheese at dinner parties.'
(Manners and Rules of Good Society 1888)

Middle class families crammed their living rooms with as many ornaments and pieces of furniture as they possibly could. Servants responsible for dusting these rooms must have hated them with a vengeance!

FATHERS AND MOTHERS

Middle class family life was ruled by the father. He earned the money which was needed to feed his family and made most of the important decisions relating to them. Middle class wives were expected to obey their husbands, look after their children and organise the day-to-day running of their homes. Some wives also helped their husbands run the family business. Others just helped their maid with the household chores. Those wives with more than one servant often found themselves with nothing to do each day but call on friends, play the piano and make endless bits and pieces for the home.

Many unmarried girls from poor families went to work as live-in servants. Their chores included lugging heavy scuttles of coal upstairs for fires, and washing their employers' clothes by hand.

13

PRESSING PETALS

When they weren't busy bossing their servants about or chatting with friends, wealthy wives often made pressed flower arrangements.

You will need: blotting paper
• freshly picked common flowers and leaves • a wooden board
• some large heavy books • glue
• a large sewing needle • thin card
• clear varnish • paint brush

Pressing works best if you use dry, fairly flat plants.

Always try to put plants of a similar thickness on the same piece of blotting paper. Large flowers will stop the books pressing down on smaller flowers and leaves.

5. If you want to use your pressed flowers to make a greeting card or bookmark, cut the card to the right shape, glue a flower design on the front and brush some varnish over it.

▲ **1.** Lay a sheet of blotting paper on top of the wooden board. Arrange the flowers and leaves on the paper, leaving a space between each one.

2. Lay a second sheet of blotting paper over the flowers and leaves.

3. Put the board in a place where it won't be moved and pile the books on top of it.

4. After about two weeks, lift up the books and the top sheet of blotting paper and carefully remove your dried plants. Use the needle to lift them off if they are stuck.

CHILDREN AT WORK

For many of those who worked in Britain's factories, Queen Victoria's reign was a period of crippling poverty. To keep costs low, factory owners and other employers often paid unskilled workers very poor wages. This meant that whole families, including children, had to work long hours just to earn enough money to eat. One father told a government committee in 1830 that when the mills were busy his daughters worked from 3 a.m. to 10 p.m. By the time they got home the girls were so tired that they fell asleep with their supper still in their mouths.

Very young children were useful in cloth-making factories because they were small enough to crawl under machines that were still running.

WOMEN AND CHILDREN FIRST

Looking after factory machinery was an unskilled job, so many bosses preferred to employ women and children because they could be paid lower wages than men. The conditions in which these women and children worked were often dreadful. The moving parts of the machinery were rarely covered, so horrific accidents were common. And the long hours spent in dark, dusty, noisy factories meant that many children grew up weak and sickly.

Factory children were not the only young workers to suffer great hardship. Before 1842 it was legal for children under ten to work underground in dark and dangerous coal mines. And up until the 1860s and 70s, many master chimney sweeps found it easy to ignore the law and send young boys up narrow, winding chimneys to brush out the soot.

Very young children worked down coal mines, opening and shutting doors to let coal trucks through. In 1842 a seven-year-old, working down a pit in Sheffield, described his job thus: 'I stand and open and shut the door; I'm generally in the dark and sit me down against the door . . . I never see daylight now except on Sundays.' ▼

Poor parents who worked from home were helped by their children. This photograph taken towards the end of Victoria's reign shows a London mother and her children making brushes. ▼

*When my mother died I was very young
And my father sold me while yet my tongue
Could scarcely cry 'weep!' 'weep!' 'weep!'
'weep!'
So your chimneys I sweep, and in soot I sleep.*

William Blake – 'The Chimney Sweep'.

CHOP AND CHANGE

During the course of Victoria's reign, laws were passed to improve poor working conditions. Some of these laws tried to stop young children from working (see pages 28 – 9). Others tried to make factory machinery safer and to ensure that workers received sick pay. These reforms did much to improve the workers' lot and, although working conditions in many industries were still bad in 1901, they were much better than they had been in 1837.

16

CITY SLUMS

During the 1800s, many workers lived in rows of 'back-to-back' houses which were built close to the factories where they worked. Dreary, damp and overcrowded, these houses had neither piped water nor indoor toilets. Instead families had to collect their water from street taps or rivers, and share outdoor 'toilets' with their neighbours. These 'toilets' were often no more than a seat built over a pit in the ground. The smelly waste which collected in the pits was removed after dark by 'night soil men' and sold to farmers for fertiliser.

As there were no proper sewers, dirty water and human waste were often left to drain away in the streets. When this muck, along with factory waste, seeped into the water supplies, those that drank the water often caught dreadful diseases like cholera and typhoid.

Smoke from factory chimneys, railways and household chimney pots made city slums dark and grimy. According to one Victorian reformer smoke made London 'the unsightliest metropolis in Europe'. ▼

CLEANING UP

As the Victorian age progressed, the government took steps to improve workers' living conditions. Underground pipes were built beneath the streets to carry away sewage, and town councils were made responsible for collecting refuse, re-developing slum areas and supplying clean drinking water. Since illness spread by city pollution sometimes threatened those living outside slum areas, the rich benefited from these changes too.

Workers' houses were shockingly overcrowded. Sometimes an entire family had to live in just one room.

SCHOOLDAYS

In early Victorian times, many children did not go to school. A variety of schools were provided for them, but since schooling was not compulsory, and rarely free, many poor children did not attend.

SCHOOL RULES

After 1870 the government set up schools in areas where there were none, and said that all children between the ages of five and ten had to go to school. In 1899 the school leaving age was raised to twelve. At first, most pupils attending the new schools had to take a few pence each week to pay for their education, but after 1891 all fees for these new schools were abolished.

CHALK AND TALK

Victorian school work was far from fun. Pupils learnt the 3 R's every day – Reading, wRiting and aRithmetic – and spent a lot of time either copying words written on the blackboard or writing down passages read out by their teacher. Discipline was very strict and those who dared to misbehave were often beaten with a cane or a leather strap.

One Victorian schoolmaster was so strict, he used to punish his pupils by banging their heads together. His skull-shattering career came to a sudden end, though, when his right arm became paralysed.

▲ A late Victorian school room. Can you see the slates on the long desks? Young children often scratched their work onto these thin pieces of rock using a stick of slate sharpened to a point. Older children used paper as well as slates.

◀ Victorian children learned to write by copying out sentences from copybooks. The size and shape of their letters had to be exactly the same as those printed in their copybooks.

STITCH! STITCH! STITCH!

Upper and middle class sons were often sent away to privately run, fee-paying schools. Their sisters, however, were not considered important enough to be educated properly. Instead they were usually kept at home and taught skills that might help them to attract a husband.

One of these supposed 'husband catching' skills was sewing, and girls practised their stitches by embroidering letters of the alphabet, texts or numbers. These pieces of embroidery, which could take months to complete, were called samplers.

To make your own sampler

You will need: canvas (3 holes to each centimetre is a good size) • embroidery silks or wool • pencil • tapestry needle • scissors • graph paper

1. Work out the spacing of your design on a piece of graph paper.

2. Copy your design onto the canvas using cross stitch.

3. To finish, oversew the outside edges of your sampler.

CROSS STITCH

To make a cross, pull the needle out through hole 1, and push it down through hole 2. Then bring it out through hole 3, and push it down through hole 4.

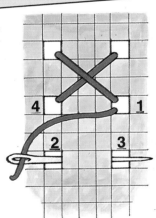

To make a second cross, bring the needle out at hole 3 and repeat as before.

OVERSEWING STITCH

Push the needle through from the back of the canvas and pull the thread through. Repeat until all the edges of your canvas are oversewn. Try to keep your stitches even.

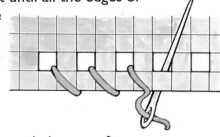

The sampler shown below was first oversewn in red, and then in green.

DOUBLE CROSS STITCH

Sew a cross stitch across three holes instead of two. Then bring the needle out at hole 1 and put it in hole 2. Bring the needle out at hole 3, and put it in hole 4.

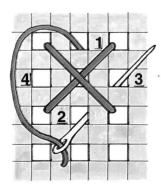

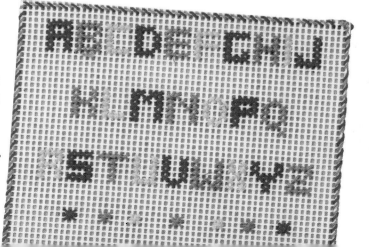

DINNER IS SERVED

With cooks and servants to prepare their food, the upper class ate very well. Their meals were served on huge dining tables, decorated with flowers and ornaments, and their cutlery, glasses and china were the very best that money could buy. Upper class dinners were often made up of many courses. For guests of the Duke of Marlborough, a dinner consisting of soup, followed by fish, followed by an entrée, followed by a meat dish, followed by a sorbet, followed by game such as pheasant or duck, followed by a dessert, followed by a hot savoury, followed by a selection of fruit . . . was not unusual!

FOOD FACTS

For the comfortably off, the Victorian age brought some welcome developments. Factories started producing kitchen equipment and coal-fired stoves which made cooking easier; by the turn of the century all major towns were linked by railway track, so fresh food could be sent quickly around the country by train; and from 1880 onwards, newly developed refrigerated steam ships brought in cheap meat, butter and fish from abroad. The arrival of cheap imported foods was good news for better-paid workers because it meant that they could afford a much more balanced diet.

Families without stoves often took their meat to the baker's shop to be cooked.

◄A middle class Victorian kitchen. Coal-fired iron stoves called ranges had ovens built into the sides and a hot surface on top for kettles and pans.

An upper class kitchen in the early 1900s. The servants shown here were only a few of those that worked in this very wealthy home.▼

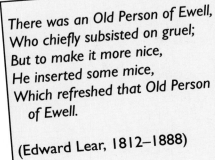

DEADLY DIET

Although the diet of many working class people had improved by the end of Victoria's reign, it was never as varied as that of the upper or middle classes. For many poor city families, meals consisted mainly of bread, potatoes, cheese, tea and porridge with perhaps a bit of bacon when they could afford it.

Worse still, until foods were properly checked for safety standards, many Victorians were at the mercy of corrupt shopkeepers who watered down their milk and added plaster to their flour and sulphuric acid to their vinegar.

MEASLY MEALS

Homeless families with nowhere to go except the parish workhouse probably had the worst diet of all. In return for work, such as breaking stones and crushing bones for glue, they were given a roof over their heads and cheap foods such as gruel. Gruel is a soup-like porridge made by boiling oatmeal in water or milk. Served with a slice of bread, it is one of the most revolting meals imaginable.

During the Victorian age, manufacturers began to use brand names and easy-to-remember symbols, so that shoppers would recognise their products. ▼

There was an Old Person of Ewell,
Who chiefly subsisted on gruel;
But to make it more nice,
He inserted some mice,
Which refreshed that Old Person of Ewell.

(Edward Lear, 1812–1888)

JUST DESSERTS

Summer puddings were very popular in Victorian times. If you would like to make one for your family or friends . . .

You will need: 675 g of mixed summer fruits, such as blackberries, blackcurrants, redcurrants, raspberries and blueberries
● 4 – 5 tablespoons of granulated sugar (more if you have a sweet tooth) ● about 9 medium slices of white bread ● a wide, heavy saucepan ● a sieve ● a soup bowl or similar ● a litre pudding basin ● a knife ● 500 g weight ● a dinner plate ● a saucer or small plate that just fits inside the top of the basin ● an old shirt or plastic apron

If you don't have a 500 g weight, use a couple of tins, paint pots, etc, that weigh 500 g or more. Serves 6 – 8.

▲ 1. Put on the apron. Remove any fruit stalks and wash the fruit.

2. Place all the fruit except the raspberries in the saucepan with the sugar. Stand the pan over a low heat and cook gently for 10 minutes, until the sugar has dissolved and the juices run. Shake the pan occasionally, but don't stir the fruit or it will lose its shape.

3. Remove the pan from the heat. Add the raspberries and leave the fruit to cool.

▲ 4. Cut the crusts off the bread. Then cut a circle of bread to fit the bottom of the pudding basin and use some of the remaining bread to line the sides. Overlap the slices of bread and press the edges together, to make sure that there are no gaps between the slices.

5. Ask an adult to help you strain the fruit and collect the juice in the soup bowl.

▲ 6. Take the bread out of the pudding basin. Quickly dip it in the juice, to colour it, and then re-line the basin.

▲ **7.** Half-fill the lined basin with fruit. Cut a circle of bread to fit the middle of the basin. Dip it in juice and place it on top of the fruit.

▲ **8.** Add the rest of the fruit and put a layer of bread, dipped in juice, on top. Trim the bread if necessary to make a nice, neat finish.

▲ **9.** Lay the small plate/saucer on top of the basin and weight it down. Put the pudding in the fridge and leave it overnight.

▲ **10.** When you are ready to eat your summer pudding, turn it out carefully onto the dinner plate. Pour over any remaining juice, cut into wedges and serve with whipped cream or thick natural yoghurt.

   If you have trouble turning out your pudding, slide a thin bladed knife around the inside of the basin, to loosen the bread.

RELIGION AND DOUBT

SOLEMN SUNDAYS

Most middle class Victorians were practising Christians. They held daily prayers at home, said grace before each meal and went to church or chapel every Sunday – sometimes two or three times. Religious families kept Sunday as a day of rest and prayer. After church, children were often expected to sing hymns, go for a walk with their parents or play quietly. In very strict households, children were not even allowed to play silent games. In fact, some families considered Sunday so holy that they turned their paintings to the wall, and spent the whole day studying and praying.

Many upper and working class Victorians were also practising Christians. Very poor families living in slums, however, didn't have time to go to church. Even if they had, they probably wouldn't have gone because they had no decent clothes to wear.

Victorian cartoons and newspapers often misunderstood Darwin's ideas and suggested that humans are descended from living apes, rather than long-extinct ones.

DARWIN'S BOMBSHELL

In 1859, a biologist called Charles Darwin stunned Christians everywhere by publishing a book which suggested that the Earth has developed slowly over millions of years, and that animal and plant species change over time. Until 1859, most Victorians believed that God had created the world in six days, as the Bible taught, and that the natural world was as it had always been. Since Darwin's scientific findings clearly went against biblical teaching, some Christians simply refused to believe his book. Others, however, were so disturbed by his ideas that they completely lost their faith in God.

THE LION OF THE SEASON.
Alarmed Flunkey. "Mr. G-G-G-O-O-O-Rilla!"

CRINOLINE CRAZY

By our standards Victorian clothes were formal and uncomfortable, particularly those worn by women and girls. To make their waists seem slim, Victorian females put on boned corsets which were sometimes pulled so tight, they felt like an instrument of torture. To make matters worse, in the 1840s and early 50s, women also wore lots of petticoats under their dresses, the weight of which must have made even the shortest stroll utterly exhausting.

During the 1850s, fashionable women of all classes abandoned some of their cloth petticoats in favour of a steel hooped underskirt called a crinoline. These cage creations, which hung from the waist like an upturned bowl, were covered with several layers of petticoat and a dress.

Crinolines varied in size from big to enormous. In fact, some of them were so huge that it was impossible for two crinolined ladies to walk into a room together without getting stuck in the

doorway. More embarrassing still, when pressure was put on one side of a crinoline's hoops, the other side shot upwards. No wonder 'respectable' women and girls wore long linen knickers under their dresses.

Blooming Cheek!
In 1851 an American called Mrs Bloomer came to England to try to persuade women to wear trousers. Her suggestion caused a storm of protest. It wasn't until the First World War (1914–1918) that wearing trousers became more acceptable for women.

SPORT AND LEISURE

In early Victorian times, working people were expected to work every day except Sundays, Christmas Day and Good Friday. In 1863, many were given Saturday afternoons off as well.

In 1871 a law was passed which allowed banks to close on Boxing Day and for one day at Easter, Whitsun and in August. As very little business could be carried out whilse the banks were shut, these four 'bank holidays' soon became public holidays.

◀ On public holidays, many families went on day trips to seaside towns such as Blackpool and Scarborough.

This is the Aston Villa team that won the F.A. cup in 1887.▼

FOOTBALL FANATICS

On their Saturday afternoons off, some workers went to the nearest public park to enjoy a bit of fresh air. Others set off to watch sporting events such as greyhound races or football matches. Until Saturday became a half day holiday, football was played mainly by public schools such as Harrow and Rugby. At first, the rules differed from school to school, especially on the question of whether players should be allowed to run holding the ball, but in 1863 the Football Association was founded and a definite set of rules were laid down. Those who agreed to these rules introduced the game to workers in industrial areas. Those who didn't played rugby instead.

The first famous football teams were founded by schools, churches, chapels and factories. Queen's Park Rangers began as a side from Droop Street School, while West Ham United was originally made up of men from the Thames Iron Works. (This is why West Ham are nick-named 'The Hammers'.) As the game became more popular, professional players were brought in, but unlike footballers today, they were paid no more than a skilled manual labourer.

Derby Day by William Frith, painted in 1858. Rich and poor people alike loved to go to the races.

HOME-MADE FUN

Without televisions, radios or CD players to keep them amused, most Victorians had to make their own home entertainment. Middle class families often played games or read to one another in the evening. Wealthy households sometimes hired musicians to come play for them, while slightly less privileged families had to put up with their own piano playing instead! Working class people enjoyed music too, and many pubs put on musical entertainments.

For those wanting a cheap and cheerful form of public entertainment, the music halls took some beating. The shows put on in these halls featured all sorts of entertainers, from dancers, comedians and singers to acrobats, magicians and conjurors. By the end of Victoria's reign, music hall performers, such as Marie Lloyd, were as rich and famous as modern pop stars.

Riddle dee dee
The Victorians loved trying to solve riddles like this one?
Q: *When is a bottle like Ireland?*

(Answer on page 30)

In Victorian times, cricket was much more popular than football. ▼

TIME LINES

INVENTIONS AND DISCOVERIES

1830s
1831 Michael Faraday makes discoveries which pave the way for electrical engineering. Two Englishmen invent the horse-drawn lawnmower.

1840s
1847 James Simpson discovers that a liquid called chloroform can be used to put patients to sleep safely during operations.

1850s
1851 Isaac Singer builds and markets the first sewing machine for use at home.

1860s
1862 By this date Louis Pasteur has discovered that disease is caused by germs. Before this discovery it was believed that many diseases were spread by smell.

IMPORTANT EVENTS

1830 First inter-city rail route opens between Liverpool and Manchester.
1837 Queen Victoria comes to the throne.
1838 Morse code is used for the first time.

1840 Adhesive postage stamps used for the first time. Penny Post begins; Victoria marries her cousin, Albert.
1845 Fungus destroys Ireland's potato crop. About 1 million people die of starvation.

1854 British soldiers go to the Crimea to help the Turks fight against Russia. Florence Nightingale goes over to nurse the soldiers and on her return starts up the first training school for nurses.
1857 India tries to gain its independence from Britain, but without success.

1860 Horse-drawn trams are used for the first time.
1863 First underground railway opens in London.
1865 London becomes one of the first cities to build proper sewers.

REFORMS

1833 Factory Act forbids children between 9 and 13 to work more than a 9-hour day.
1839 Town and county police forces are formed.

1842 Women, girls and young boys no longer allowed to work underground.
1847 Women and children under 18 can only work 10 hours a day.

1852 Great Ormond Street Hospital for Children is founded in London.

1864 Young boys are no longer allowed to work as chimney sweeps.
1868 Groups of workers join together to form an organisation called the Trades Union Congress (TUC). United in this way, workers find it easier to improve their working conditions and pay.

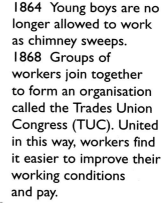

LEISURE AND PLEASURE

1838 Charles Dickens writes 'Oliver Twist'; Walter Wingfield invents a game called Sphairistike, which becomes lawn tennis.
1839 The first Grand National is run.

1841 Thomas Cook organises his first 'package' holiday from Leicester to . . . Loughborough.
1846 Edward Lear publishes his first nonsense poems.

1857 Thomas Hughes publishes his book 'Tom Brown's Schooldays'.
1859 Charles Darwin publishes his blockbuster 'On the Origin of Species'.

1863 Charles Kingsley writes 'The Water Babies', which tells the tale of a young chimney sweep who dies and comes back to life underwater.
1865 Lewis Carroll publishes his book 'Alice in Wonderland'.

1870s

1876 Alexander Graham Bell invents the telephone; Thomas Edison invents an early type of record player.
1878/9 Swan and Edison invent the electric light bulb.

1870 Elizabeth Garrett Anderson becomes the first woman to qualify as a doctor in Britain.
1877 Queen Victoria is made Empress of India by her Prime Minister.
1878 William Booth founds the Salvation Army, which ran shelters for the needy.

1870 New Board schools are built in areas where there are not enough schools.
1874 Children under nine are not allowed to go to work.
1875 Town councils are made responsible for street cleaning and the supply of clean water.

1871 Bank Holidays are introduced.
1872 First ever FA Cup Final.
1873 Start of the cricket county championships.
1877 First Lawn Tennis Championship is played at Wimbledon.

1880s

1882 Robert Koch discovers the germ which causes tuberculosis. This was the first step towards discovering a cure for this deadly disease.
1886 Coca Cola is invented in America.

1880 Cragside in Northumbria becomes the first house in the world to be lit by electricity.
1885 Karl Benz builds the first petrol-powered car.
1888 A mysterious murderer, nick-named Jack the Ripper, terrorises London.

1880 All children have to go to school until they are 10.
1882 Women are allowed to keep any wealth they are given as a gift or an inheritance. Before this a woman's husband was entitled to this wealth.

1888 Football league is founded.

1890s

1893 Rudolph Diesel builds the first diesel engine. Diesel engines, which burn oil as fuel, are more efficient than steam-powered engines. Many modern vehicles have diesel engines.

1890 Opening of the Forth Bridge in Scotland, the world's first large steel structure; electric trams come onto the rails for the first time.
1895 X-rays are demonstrated for the first time.
1899 Boer War begins. Britons win this three year war against the Boers in South Africa, and Boer territory becomes part of the British Empire.

1891 Minimum working age is raised to 11; primary education in Board schools is made free.
1899 Children must stay on at school until they are 12.

1896 First modern Olympic Games.

1900s

1907 Bakelite, the first modern plastic is invented.
1908 Cellophane is invented.

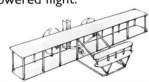

The first diesel engine

1900 The Labour Party is officially founded. Until the 1900s British politics was dominated by the Conservative and Liberal Parties.
1901 Queen Victoria dies and her son, Edward VII, comes to the throne.
1903 The Wright Brothers make the first powered flight.

1902 Rudyard Kipling writes his 'Just So Stories'.

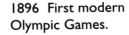

GLOSSARY

Arithmetic – maths

Back-to-back – a house which backs onto another house so that neither of them has a back yard

Biologist – a scientist who studies living things

Census – an official count of population. A census has been taken in Britain every ten years since 1801, except for 1941, when Britain was at war with Germany

Embankment – a mound built to carry a level road or railway over a low-lying place

Empire – a wide-spread group of lands ruled by one powerful country

Entrée – a dish served at dinner between the main courses

Industrial nation – a country in which large amounts of goods are made in factories

Industry – a trade which produces large quantities of goods

Manufacturer – someone who makes goods on a large scale

Memorial – a statue, pillar, tomb, etc, built in memory of a person or an event

Metropolis– the capital of a country

Mill – a type of factory

Monarch – a king or queen

Smelt – to melt (one) in order to separate metal from other material

Sorbet – a frozen dessert made from fruit, water and sugar

Transformation – a change

Answers:
page 7 **a. 151.5 km/h** Average speed is worked out by dividing distance (303 km) by the time it takes to travel that distance (2 hours).

   b. 55 km We know the average speed of the 1840 train was approximately 27.5 km/h. Therefore, in 2 hours passengers would have travelled 2 x 27.5 = 55 km.

page 27 **A: *When it has a Cork in it!***

PLACES TO VISIT

Here is a list of just some of the many British museums which have exhibits from the Victorian period. If you want further information about the museums in your area, contact your local tourist board. If you want to find out whether there are any Victorian buildings in your neighbourhood, go to your local history museum or reference library. The staff there should be able to help you find what you're looking for.

Beamish, North of England Open Air Museum
Beamish,
County Durham,
DH9 0RG
Tel: (0207) 231811

Bethnal Green Museum of Childhood
Cambridge Heath Road,
London E2 9PA
Tel: 081 989 2415

Bradford Industrial Museum
Moorside Mills,
Moorside Road,
Eccleshill,
Bradford,
West Yorkshire,
BD2 3HP
Tel: (0274) 631756

Cookworthy Museum
The Old Grammar School,
108 Fore Street,
Kingsbridge,
Devon
Tel: (0548) 853235

Ironbridge Gorge Museum
Ironbridge, Telford, Shropshire
Tel: (0952) 433522 (weekdays),
(0952) 432166 (weekends)

Museum of Childhood
42 High Street, Edinburgh
Tel: 031 225 2424

Museum of London
London Wall,
London EC2Y 5HN
Tel: 071 600 3699

National Railway Museum
Leeman Road,
York YO2 4XJ
Tel: 0904 621261

Nottingham Industrial Museum
Courtyard Buildings,
Wollaton Park,
Nottingham NG8 2AE
Tel: (0602) 284602

Ulster Folk and Transport Museum,
Witham Street Gallery,
Belfast BT4 1HP
Tel: 0232 451519

Welsh Folk Museum
St Fagans, South Glamorgan,
CF5 6XB
Tel: 0222 569441

York Castle Museum
The Eye of York,
York, YO1 1RY
Tel: (0904) 653611

Yorkshire Mining Museum
Caphouse Colliery,
New Road, Overton,
Wakefield WF4 4RH
Tel: (0924) 848806

INDEX

Additional Photographs: Bradford Industrial Museum P. 13; e.t. archive P. 27; Hulton-Deutsch Picture Library P. 8, 13, 21, 25; J. Allan Cash Ltd P. 6, 11, 21; The Mansell Collection P. 4, 9; Mary Evans Picture Library P. 7, 10, 11, 15, 24, 26; National Trust P. 5, 12; Robert Oppie Collection P. 21; Salvation Army International Heritage Centre P. 16; Warwickshire Museum P. 18.

Contents

Contents

Context

A substantial number of young people have motor co-ordination and perceptual difficulties affecting their participation in class activities. These *may* have been identified during their primary years on the evidence of poor handwriting legibility, erratic organisation in the classroom, or difficulties with reading, mathematics and physical education. These pupils' struggles may also have had an impact on self-image, reflected in limitations in artwork and in personal appearance. As a consequence, academic success, peer relationships, social skills and self-confidence may all have been affected. In the secondary-school years these issues are felt more keenly owing to the desire to fit in and to be accepted by a potentially large, and often unforgiving, peer group.

The structure of secondary education demands that students are well organised, self-sufficient and increasingly autonomous learners, who can cope with a diverse timetable referring to buildings that may appear vast when compared to their primary school. They are also required to remember the name, and subject speciality, of between ten and fifteen teachers who may work with up to a thousand or more children, in contrast to their primary school where there may have been only one or two significant figures, consistently located in a recognised classroom, teaching an array of subjects to them for a year or more.

It is essential that the needs of young people with co-ordination difficulties in secondary education are understood in order that strategies can be put in place so that both their transition into and experience of secondary education are positive, enabling each one to reach their potential and fulfil career aspirations.

Dyspraxia Foundation,
8 West Alley, Hitchin,
Hertfordshire, SG5 1EG

www.dyspraxiafoundation.org.uk

The combination of perceptual and motor difficulties experienced by children and young people was previously termed 'dyspraxia'. The universally accepted term 'developmental co-ordination disorder' or DCD has been introduced to help focus research and resources in the appropriate direction.

The information in this book is intended to inspire teachers and health care professionals to:

- ● understand the unique needs of young people with DCD;
- ● understand why young people with DCD have difficulties in perceptual and motor planning;
- ● appreciate the impact of DCD on learning;
- ● consider the influence of peer pressure and puberty on DCD;
- ● provide practical strategies to help;
- ● consider post-16 and vocational training.

It is also intended to help parents/carers of young people with DCD to understand the help that is available to their child as they make the transition into secondary education.

Chapter 1
Common questions about DCD

What is DCD?

Childhood conditions are typically defined by two medical bodies: the American Psychiatric Association and the World Health Organization (WHO). These are professional bodies which, after extensive consultation, identify explicit characteristics that collectively identify a specific condition. The purpose of this is to help researchers and clinicians identify the causes and research strategies to support those whose development may be different from others. Currently both organisations are revising their criteria.

The proposed definition for DCD encompasses three criteria:

1   Motor performance that is *substantially below* expected levels, given the person's chronological age and previous opportunities for skill acquisition.

   o   Poor motor performance that may manifest as co-ordination problems, poor balance, clumsiness, dropping or bumping into things.

   o   Marked delays in achieving developmental motor milestones (e.g. walking, crawling and sitting).

   o   Difficulty in acquiring basic motor skills (e.g. catching, throwing, kicking, running, jumping, hopping, cutting, colouring, printing, writing).

2   These difficulties significantly interfere with activities of daily living or academic achievement.

3   The motor co-ordination difficulties are not due to a general medical condition (e.g. cerebral palsy, hemiplegia, muscular dystrophy).

Having dyspraxia feels like I have got my feet on backwards and every time I have a goal and try to walk to it, I start walking backwards.

It is important to note that these traits relate to an individual who typically has average or above-average intelligence and does not have global developmental delay. There will be an observable difference between the young person's cognitive ability and skills requiring motor and perceptual processing. Teachers will notice a difference between the student's written and verbal performance, the latter being considerably better than the former.

In adolescence these traits continue to be apparent. Walking will appear laboured and slower than average, with evidence of more sway or swagger than is usual. Running may look awkward, effortful and cumbersome, with limited speed and inability to initiate planned movements. Difficulties in throwing, catching, kicking and jumping will become increasingly evident as physical education becomes more competitive, focusing on team sports and games such as netball, hockey, athletics, cricket and football.

Embarrassment will occur when creative tasks are undertaken, with colouring, drawing and painting skills appearing immature and somewhat basic. The handwriting difficulties experienced in the early years will continue to be an issue as the pressure to increase speed and volume increases, causing legibility to become more problematic.

As criterion 2 states, the motor and perceptual processing difficulties also affect activities of daily living. These include an awareness of appearance, hygiene, using a knife and fork with ease, co-ordinating colours and deciding on clothing combinations. These are significant problems where teenagers are concerned, and individuals may be acutely aware that the way they process, present and record information in relation to these is different from that of their peers, but be unable or unsure about how to change this.

Although students with DCD are usually identified in their primary years, some may slip through the net. Subsequently they may be something of an anathema to professionals working in the secondary setting. Teachers will state that there seems to be a mismatch in their abilities. Time management, general organisation and poor attention may be evident, resulting in important information being missed.

Although the medical criteria described earlier help to differentiate one developmental condition from another, ultimately the term or label is unimportant. What is important is how the student functions, and which strategies can be put into place to maximise their learning opportunities. When we see how an individual functions in a variety of contexts, it is possible to see whether the individual, the system or the environment is influencing the learning process, helping to focus strategies on the most appropriate issue.

How many young people have DCD?

Online teen forums include:
www.dyspraxicteens.org.uk/forum/index.php
www.hdcd.org.uk
www.dyspraxiadcdcork.ie/tips_teens.pdf

Recent research in the UK has identified that 1.7 per cent of the population have DCD and a further 3.2 per cent have probable DCD, depending on the assessments used (Lingam *et al.* 2009). Therefore we can assume that in a class of approximately 25 students at least one will have motor co-ordination and perceptual difficulties which will affect their learning and will warrant extra support. DCD affects boys more than girls; boys are four times more likely than girls to be referred for assessment, therapy and specialist teaching.

What causes DCD?

The causes of DCD remain unclear. It is likely that multiple factors give rise to the symptoms. The following are examples of current thinking:

- Differences in **brain structure** during early development (Querne *et al.* 2008).
- **Prematurity** may result in poor motor co-ordination such as that seen in children with DCD (Foulder-Hughes and Cooke 2003; Marlow *et al.* 2005).
- DCD may be the result of an inability to integrate different **sensory information**, which provides a mental understanding of the body and limb position, essential for motor planning (Piek *et al.* 2004). The poor integration

of sensory information causes children to react differently to touch, movement, sights, smells, and so on and has a considerable bearing on functional performance, particularly in the classroom (Davies and Gavin 2007).

Is there a link between DCD and other developmental conditions?

It has become increasingly evident that there is an overlap between DCD and other developmental conditions. When this connection occurs, the term 'comorbidity' or 'co-occurrence' is used. Recent research has found that there are symptoms that may co-exist with DCD, these being difficulty in focusing or sustaining attention and/or poor social interaction. Therefore young people with DCD may also show traits of ADHD and/or autism; they may have dyslexia or dyscalculia too. The use of two terms – such as DCD with ADHD – may be very confusing and leave parents and teachers exasperated about which direction to turn to for help. Once again the emphasis must be placed on the child's functional requirements, not the diagnostic criteria.

How does DCD present?

Individuals with DCD have difficulty with preparing and organising themselves to perform a given task; the comprehension of a task may be satisfactory but the visualisation, planning and execution may be dysfunctional. Motor and perceptual information becomes disorganised owing to a number of factors: poor sensory information, deficient visuo–spatial skills, inadequate proprioceptive feedback, and so on. Therefore it is not the motor skills per se that are influencing performance – as in, for example, cerebral palsy or muscular dystrophy (although children with DCD often have low muscle tone or hypotonia). Rather it is impaired processing that is interfering with motor co-ordination.

The checklist opposite shows characteristics of secondary-school age students with DCD, and will help you identify specific features, all of which have a profound effect on self-esteem and academic achievement.

Do young people 'grow out' of DCD?

It is not possible to grow out of DCD, and there is evidence that 70 per cent of individuals diagnosed with DCD in childhood continue to have difficulties into adulthood (Kirby et al. 2008). This may impact on activities such as learning to drive, engagement in sport, participation in higher education, riding a bicycle and social integration. The remaining 30 per cent have learned, with help, to compensate positively for their processing differences.

However, this does not mean the outlook is pessimistic. With support and understanding, young people with DCD can have a full and active adult life, with similar employment opportunities to those of their peers.

Books by teenagers to help people understand their experiences include:

Caged in Chaos: A Dyspraxic Guide to Breaking Free, by Victoria Biggs. Jessica Kingsley Publishers, 2005.

Living with Dyspraxia: A Guide for Adults with Developmental Dyspraxia, by Mary Colley, Victoria Biggs and Amanda Kirby. Jessica Kingsley Publishers, 2006.

That's the Way I Think, by David Grant. David Fulton Publishers, 2010.

Characteristics of secondary students with DCD

Characteristic	Evidence	Some evidence	No evidence
Poor manipulation affecting the speed of dressing/undressing before and after sport and PE.			
Poor organisation of clothing – i.e. clothes may be worn back to front or inside out.			
Poor understanding of how to co-ordinate clothing, manage hair care and control appearance, affecting street cred and peer relationships.			
Frequent tripping up and bumping. (Note that it is usual for young boys to become uncoordinated during puberty, owing to their rapidly changing body schema; the clumsiness experienced by children with DCD is in excess of this.)			
Poor ball skills, affecting participation in sports such as football and cricket.			
Difficulties in performing bilateral activities such as sewing, using scissors, fastening buttons, tying shoe laces and using a knife and fork.			
Poor self-awareness.			
Confusion between left and right.			
Poor drawing skills, noticeable in art lessons.			
Poor constructional skills, especially noted in design/technology.			
Difficulties in design/technology with poor conceptualisation of three dimensions.			
Inability to write quickly and legibly.			
Difficulty in copying text from a book, whiteboard or blackboard.			
Scant written content despite evidence of knowledge through discussion.			
Difficulties in taking dictation or recalling detailed instructions; this may be due to poor auditory figure–ground discrimination, affecting the student's short-term memory.			
Presentation and organisation of calculations in mathematics is messy and confused.			
Frustration when several things are happening at once.			
Distraction/daydreaming.			
Short attention span and/or difficulty in concentrating.			
May be a loner.			
May be disruptive in class.			
Heavy footed and ham fisted.			
May get into trouble for being overenthusiastic when meeting people – a hug may be too strong, and a pat on the back may cause friends to feel winded.			
Increasingly conscious and aware that they are not performing at the same level as that of peers, but not sure what to do about this.			
General disorganisation and forgetfulness.			
Poor appreciation of personal space.			

Chapter 2
Understanding DCD
and how it affects learning

Students with DCD are typically recognised by their lack of motor co-ordination. They are often heavy footed and seem to bump into everything. They are physically awkward and are reluctant to participate in PE lessons, quickly developing strategies for avoiding activities that appear too challenging. In order to address their needs, it is important to understand why they have these difficulties. That helps us to appreciate the struggles and adjustments that they have to make on a daily basis.

Proprioception

Proprioception is the awareness of where your limbs are in space. Located inside our muscles and joints are sensitive receptors that react to the amount of muscle movement we make. These receptors inform our brain about how much the muscle is responding, and the information is recorded for future use in our memory system. This helps us to develop controlled limb movements. Proprioceptors are located all over our body, together providing us with a mental map of our whole body's position. They help us to form a body schema (a mental impression of what our body looks like and an understanding of where each limb is in relation to the rest of our body). This enables us to perform actions we cannot see, such as brushing the back of our hair, cleaning ourselves after toileting and tucking in clothes.

Students with DCD have poor proprioception; the messages they receive through their muscles, joints and tendons are inaccurate. This causes them to place objects with too much strength, or to become overreliant on vision to compensate for a lack of controlled sensation. This is the start of the individual appearing clumsy.

As a consequence of poor muscle feedback, there is a craving for a sensory response. That craving causes the individual to wriggle or to be heavy handed and/or heavy footed. This is a natural response for all of us. For example, if you lie or sit too long in one position your leg or arm tends to 'fall asleep'. It becomes numb, the lack of muscle feedback makes you feel unsteady and lacking in control, so you rub the area concerned or stamp your feet until the usual sensation has returned. By doing this you are stimulating the proprioceptors in order to help regain motor control. In DCD this kind of behaviour is common. Students with reduced limb sensation will resort to stomping, squashing and leaning against an object or person; and to wriggling, rocking and pressing in order to gain the feedback that they crave.

Poor proprioception is also responsible for the inability to monitor muscle effort or inertia. This may be seen when students with DCD throw a ball. They are unable to control the effort needed to throw accurately, and the ball is either projected too far or too near. Similarly the force to kick a football may be inappropriate. This can impact on these students' success in sports such as cricket, football and hockey. Bat and ball games may be particularly problematic.

Vestibular system

The vestibular apparatus is located in the semi-circular canals within our inner ear and gives us information regarding balance, direction and the velocity of movement. When this system is altered, the first symptom is a loss of balance; then comes a feeling of nausea, uncertainty and lack of coordination. This will often be appreciated when you suffer from an ear infection. In this situation, it is preferable to sit down or reduce movement as far as possible. Thankfully, an ear infection is temporary, but for those with DCD, it is often their day-to-day experience: movement is fraught with insecurity. This is particularly true when moving up and down stairs between lessons, when difficulty is exacerbated by the volume of students. This can explain the preference of people with DCD for sitting down, and for participating in sedentary activities rather than ones that require them to be upright or mobile.

Sensory system

The sensory system is a further way of providing detailed information about our environment. There are numerous specialised receptors that are responsible for this task; these include receptors that focus on vision, light, temperature, touch, hearing, taste and smell. Young people with DCD may have reduced sensitivity, particularly with regard to touch, taste and smell, and will therefore become overreliant on their strongest sense: vision. Alternatively they may be oversensitive to sensory input and be adverse to certain noises, tastes and tactile and visual experiences. This fluctuation in tolerance is known as **sensory modulation**, and may explain some of the distinctive features associated with DCD.

The proprioception, vestibular and sensory systems interact and help us to develop perception. In young people with DCD there will be sensory integration difficulties, resulting in differences in perceptual processing. These particularly affect the following.

Hand–eye co-ordination

Hand–eye co-ordination – or visual motor co-ordination as it is often termed – is the ability to place the hand in relation to a target. Dysfunctional proprioception and vestibular feedback causes incorrect information to be given about the location of the arm and hand, and the degree of movement required to reach an object. This results in poor judgement of space and imprecise motor skills. It will make even the simplest of tasks difficult – for example, fastening a tie, using a knife and fork, and positioning a ruler. This in turn has an effect on self-esteem and causes some students to avoid certain tasks.

Poor hand–eye co-ordination also results in more reliance on vision to guide motor control. This slows down the process and causes movements to become disjointed and prone to error. This may be appreciated when we consider driving a car. When we learn to drive, each task is introduced by the instructor, then reiterated and practised until it becomes automatic. The initial overt recitation of 'mirror, signal, and manoeuvre' quickly becomes a series of subconscious actions and habitual once the learner has completed a significant amount of driving. It is only when an interruption occurs, perhaps in the form of criticism or awareness of a potential accident, that the individual steps are overtly remembered. Then driving becomes a more conscious process, and lacks automaticity. The return to step-by-step processes may make the action appear fragmented and awkward, and hinder co-ordinated movements.

Visual form constancy

Perceptual constancy is the ability to perceive an object as possessing variant properties, such as shape, position, colour, tone and size. The recognition of three-dimensional objects requires multiple sensory experiences, including vision and touch. Perceptual constancy helps in forming an understanding of the properties of a given object and so, for example, enables an individual to recognise a mug, even when it is viewed from an unusual angle, or a table viewed from a number of different angles. This experience not only helps in the recognition of objects but also in awareness of the size of the object.

Young people with DCD receive the wrong information regarding touch, weight, texture and visual dimension owing to poor proprioception and diminished tactile feedback. This may make the recognition of familiar objects presented in an unfamiliar way problematic. The student may be unable to order the sizes and forms they have previously viewed, and if this happens their environment will appear extremely unstable. A similar object may appear completely different in altered circumstances, even slightly changed ones. For example, in sport the football that is recognised as one size in a near location may appear totally different from a distance. Consequently when a ball is kicked towards a student with DCD, they may be unable to adjust to the actual size of the ball. A calculator placed at the front of a classroom may look completely different from one held in the hand.

A table viewed from a number of angles

Perception of objects

by Roger Shepard

Statues or balustrade?

Visual figure–ground discrimination

Figure–ground discrimination is the ability to select and focus on one item or object while disregarding the mass of stimuli within an environment. The figure is the focus of the visual field that accommodates the observer's attention. When the attention is shifted on to something different, the previous figure recedes into the background.

When a young person has distorted figure–ground perception everything they see has equal importance and therefore it is difficult to maintain focus on one specific object. This causes visual and auditory attention difficulties. It also has a profound effect on organisation, so necessary in the secondary-school environment.

Reaction to overload of information can vary from person to person. Some students simply 'switch off' and wait for the teacher to repeat information, others become more frustrated and 'act out' so that they are removed from the work they are expected to do.

Position in space

Position in space involves the ability to perceive or view oneself in relation to another object or person. It also incorporates the understanding of spatial concepts such as above, below, beneath and around, and the appreciation of where things are placed in relation to a central figure. The appreciation of self in relation to another requires an accurate body schema. We have learned that this is a sense of where your body is in space – for example, where the arms are in relation to the trunk, where the legs are, and the orientation of the trunk. All these provide a map or picture of how we think we look. It is through this information that we can perceive ourselves as symmetrical and appropriately proportioned. We can also appreciate laterality: the sense of right and left.

Students with DCD may have a disordered body schema owing to poor proprioceptive, tactile, kinaesthetic and sensory feedback. This will have an effect on figure drawing, understanding proportion and, subsequently, personal appearance; shirts will often be left untucked and tidiness will be compromised. Distorted perception may also cause clothes to be put on inside out or back to front, shoes to be put on the wrong feet, and shirt buttons to be misaligned while being fastened. Poor recognition of left and right may affect map reading in geography, orientation around the school and, later, learning to drive.

Spatial relationships

Spatial relationship is concerned with the ability to perceive the position of two or more objects in relation to the self and in relation to each other. Spatial understanding involves the need for accurate visual memory as several items must be visualised, remembered and recalled simultaneously to organise the action necessary. For example, when playing goalkeeper in football, the whole field can be scanned and a picture made up of exactly where all the players are, how far they are from each other, and how far from the goal. In this way preparation can be made to move swiftly into the most appropriate position.

Difficulties in spatial organisation are common in students with DCD. This is why they seem to bump into things frequently and to appear clumsy. Difficulties in this area of visual perception will affect the individual's ability to write: spaces will be omitted between words, writing may commence from the centre of the page, and it may be carried out in a diagonal direction rather than horizontally. Mathematics may prove problematic as the presentation and layout of calculations may easily be misplaced, thus affecting the end result.

Visual closure

Visual closure is an area of perception and relates to an object being identified when only a part of the object can be seen. Difficulties in visual closure will present in construction tasks, and in general classroom organisation. The student may struggle to identify a book or required piece of apparatus if it is only partially in view.

Example of visual closure.
Can you read the words?

Visual and auditory memory

The term 'memory' is used to define the encoding, storage and later retrieval of knowledge. Students with DCD may struggle to process and retain information, not simply because of a memory deficit, but because of their inability to process several items of information at once. They will find that the use of multisensory rehearsal techniques and overlearning is necessary. Interestingly, they may be able to learn selected facts very well – in the quietness of a bedroom, they may be able to absorb facts that are of interest to them, such as the names of all the players in a football team. However, recalling what to do for homework may be more problematic. This reflects the importance of context; when several actions are going on at once, the student may struggle to remember essential detail.

In the early stages of child development it is possible to introduce children to a carefully selected variety of sensory experiences in order to enhance and improve their perceptual acuity. However, as the child grows older motor skills, memory and visual and auditory perception become increasingly difficult to alter. The student then begins to adopt compensatory strategies. Some of these are helpful and subtle and hide their difficulties; others are more negative and are associated with emerging behaviours that appear peculiar or disruptive. It is therefore important to observe carefully the approaches adopted by young people to identify whether further guidance or alternative techniques should be introduced.

Chapter 3
Assessment at Key Stages 3 and 4

Formal assessment

A child with DCD usually comes to the attention of professionals at the age of 6 or 7, when they have settled into full-time education. They will quickly be seen to lack motor co-ordination and have verbal skills that are far more advanced than their manual abilities (unless they have oral dyspraxia).

If the child is referred to the local Child Development Centre, a detailed assessment of the child's perceptual, cognitive and motor skills will be carried out, along with a review of the child's abilities in daily living skills, and of their emotional well-being. Strategies will be put into place within the school and targeted developmental programmes may be introduced, such as handwriting programmes, motor activity sessions and interventions relating to teaching activities for daily living.

At secondary school formal assessment is more problematic. The reason for instigating the assessment process needs to be clear. The student will have coped for 11 or more years with their co-ordination differences and will have adopted many compensatory strategies, positive and negative. Observation will help to identify behaviours or tactics that are being used to compensate for poor motor and perceptual processing. Formal assessment will only be undertaken for the following reasons:

- Evidence for extra time in examinations.
- Evidence that an alternative to handwriting is necessary.
- Appreciation that different time scales for homework are appropriate.
- An alternative assessment method is needed.
- An understanding of the individual's peculiarities.

Movement Assessment Battery for Children (MABC-2; Sugden et al. 2007)

The main assessment tool for determining motor co-ordination difficulties is the *Movement Assessment Battery for Children*. This measures three aspects of motor co-ordination using eight simple tasks, some of which are timed. Band 3 of this test assesses students aged 11 to 16 years:

Manual dexterity	• Turning pegs over and placing them into a pegboard, one-handed • Completing a triangular structure using nuts and bolts • Bicycle trail (a narrow tracking exercise)
Aiming and catching	• One-hand catch • Throwing at a wall target
Balance	• Two-board balance • Zig-zag hopping • Walking backwards

DCDQ'07: free access through the following website
http://www.dcdq.ca

If there is a query about whether an individual has DCD or not, the DCDQ'07 (Wilson *et al.* 2007), for those aged 5 to 15 years, may be undertaken without the student being referred to a GP or paediatrician. The DCDQ'07 is an online questionnaire which offers statements such as 'Your child throws a ball in a controlled and accurate fashion' and asks the parent/carer to score this from 1 to 5. It may be completed by the child themself. Access to it is free.

There is also a free downloadable questionnaire specifically for young adults written by Rosenbaum and Kirby (2008). This, too, is accessible online.

Rosenbaum and Kirby's questionnaire is accessible online at
http://ebookbrowse.com/the-questionnaire-the-adult-dcd-dyspraxia-checklist-pdf-d85251399

Further assessments may be undertaken by a specialist teacher, an occupational therapist or an educational psychologist, to support learning or provide evidence in support of examination concessions, or to provide a focus for an individual education plan (IEP) or provision map.

Following assessment, a **graduated approach** to support may be applied, depending on the extent of the student's difficulties.

Graduated approach to DCD

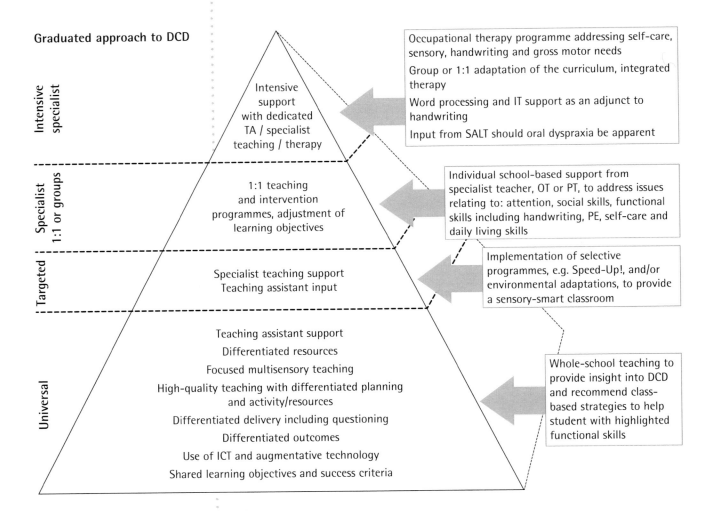

Intensive specialist

Intensive support with dedicated TA / specialist teaching / therapy

> Occupational therapy programme addressing self-care, sensory, handwriting and gross motor needs
>
> Group or 1:1 adaptation of the curriculum, integrated therapy
>
> Word processing and IT support as an adjunct to handwriting
>
> Input from SALT should oral dyspraxia be apparent

Specialist 1:1 or groups

1:1 teaching and intervention programmes, adjustment of learning objectives

> Individual school-based support from specialist teacher, OT or PT, to address issues relating to: attention, social skills, functional skills including handwriting, PE, self-care and daily living skills

Targeted

Specialist teaching support
Teaching assistant input

> Implementation of selective programmes, e.g. Speed-Up!, and/or environmental adaptations, to provide a sensory-smart classroom

Universal

Teaching assistant support
Differentiated resources
Focused multisensory teaching
High-quality teaching with differentiated planning and activity/resources
Differentiated delivery including questioning
Differentiated outcomes
Use of ICT and augmentative technology
Shared learning objectives and success criteria

> Whole-school teaching to provide insight into DCD and recommend class-based strategies to help student with highlighted functional skills

OT = occupational therapist
PT = physiotherapist
SALT = speech and language therapist

Provision maps

Provision maps are now regularly used in schools to detail the range of support and specific programmes that can be provided to students with DCD at the different stages of intervention. These show at a glance the range of staffing, specialist programmes and other support that may be required. The chart on page 18 gives an example of a wave-based provision map for secondary school students with DCD. The list provided is by no means exhaustive and should be added to when proven programmes/interventions become known.

In addition, many authorities use a provision map, such as that shown on page 19, to formulate the cost of a student's needs. An advantage of this approach is that, unlike Individual Education Plans (IEPs), a provision map doesn't have to be rewritten for every child. This reduces the amount of paperwork required.

Although the kind of provision map shown on page 18 is an excellent way of informing teachers about the options available to them to help selected pupils, it does not include measurable targets. IEPs provide goals to which students with DCD may aspire. These should be SMART (specific, measurable, achievable, realistic and time measured). Many teachers now add the student's specific targets to the provision map.

An example of an IEP for a student aged 12 years with DCD and attention/ behavioural issues is shown on pages 20–21. Usually three to four targets are established each term; however the year's targets have been included on the sample plan to demonstrate the variety of needs being addressed.

Much to the annoyance of everyone I always look a mess because I wear comfy baggy clothes that take a minute or two to put on and I'm ready. I always forget to brush my hair and I hate make-up and don't want to try it so I don't wear it. I always wear male clothes so everything is too big for me and I can slip any buttoned clothes on and off. Though I've gone to wearing elasticated sweatpants which are even easier to put on, and my trainers are super easy to put on due to Velcro now. I just get them and my slippers on the wrong feet quite often.

I was always the last out of the changing rooms and I used to pretend I'd forgotten my kit just so I didn't have to do it. And in swimming, too! I always had to walk back with my friend because I was too slow to catch the minibus with everyone.

Provision map for students with DCD

Universal: quality first teaching	Targeted intervention and support for groups	Intensive personalised/individualised learning
Sensory smart strategies	Class teacher and TA offer planned support and interventions including the following:	An individual provision map and termly IEP education which may include the following:
Structure/routine and consistency at all times with visual-symbol timetable	Reinforcing learning and developing the ability to reflect, recall and consolidate learning experiences	Provision of a key worker who may not be a teacher
Appropriate expectations of written work, such as decreasing the motor (output) of the task, without changing the cognitive expectations	Modelling and coaching for individual pupils – related to targets	Intensive handwriting programme and/or word-processing training
Adequate/extra time and assistance for written tasks	Functional motor skills work, e.g. design technology, home economics.	Programmes to develop auditory attention, such as the Listening programme®
Accommodation of handwriting presentation	Selected small-group sports activities.	Application of sensory integration techniques such as the Alert programme
ICT support / technological aids to record work, e.g. Dictaphone™, word prediction software	Social skills training to increase appropriate social interactions	Literacy Plus programmes
Differentiated curriculum with multisensory learning experiences	Help with organisational skills, e.g. visual/symbolic timetable, school map, mobile phone reminders	Fitness training / personal trainer support (teacher, TA or buddy)
Appropriate teaching styles that match identified learning style of the student	Expressive and receptive language support within a group to improve social skills.	Organisational strategies and memory training
Simple, short/small-step instructions, repeated and prompted with possible visual clues MATCH (Modify the task, Alter expectations, Teach strategies, Change the environment, Help the student by understanding their difficulties)	Alternative strategies to promote progress in reading, spelling, writing, e.g. spell-checks, mobile notes	Strategies to develop self-help skills, e.g. dressing before and after PE
Subtle visual prompts and reminders	Group or individualised aid, e.g. task diary, homework diary, appointment apps	ICT skill acquisition / increased use of ICT (Dictaphone, voice-activated software, predictive software, phone apps, iPad)
Differentiated homework policy	Alternatives to written recording, e.g. video, voice recording, iPad applications, Dragon Naturally Speaking	Teach keyboard shortcuts instead of using mouse, sticky keys, tracker ball or wireless mouse
Peer and buddy support	Enhance the use of ICT, e.g. introduce screen filters to cut down glare, increase font sizes for screen, ensure the use of a clear font type (Arial or Comic Sans), provide appropriate contrast between background and text	Subject area or curriculum area specific tutorials
	Ensure that fonts in printed material are not smaller than 12 point (24 point for screen presentations)	Counselling where appropriate
	Introduce a talking word processor to read out text	Guidance on issues relating to adolescence, e.g. relationships, sex, interpreting social cues, personal presentation
	Visual thinking methods, e.g. mind maps	Provision of memory aids
	Small-group catch-up/other intervention programmes as appropriate, e.g. literacy workshops, Literacy Plus programmes	Differentiated homework, accepting alternative assessment methods
	Planned activities during unstructured times for socialisation / gross motor skills development	Teaching study skills
	Providing opportunities / encouragement to join lunchtime or homework clubs	Summer school workshops
		Close liaison with parents as supported by Achievement for All
		Work experience opportunities (more than their peers so that students can appreciate the demands of the workplace while helping to identify career aspirations)
		Practical living skills training, e.g. budgeting, using public transport, meal preparation
		Preparation for higher or further education
		Transition planning

Provision map with frequency

Year	Provision resource	Individual or group	Cost in time (per week)	Term / no. of weeks to run
7	Support for subject staff in implementing modified environment/materials / differentiation SENCo/TA + subject staff Rolling programme working within specialist subject: English language and literature, art and design / DT, PE, maths approx. 4 weeks	Individual	1 x 1 hour per week with SENCo	All year
	Whole-school Insight training Key Stages 3 and 4	Group	2 x 1 hour session per term with SENCo	Autumn term, summer term
	Lunchtime support / homework club	Group (approx. 15)	2 x 1 hour per week, supervised by TA	All year
	Physical literacy course	Group (approx. 15)	1 x 1 hour per week, led by 2 TAs	All year
	1:1 literacy/word-processing training Withdrawn from negotiated lessons	Individual (10 pupils in IT suite)	Initial 1 hour session to introduce programme, with teacher, then independent practice, with supervision given by TA	Two terms
	Numeracy groups (during maths lessons)	2 groups of 4	Initial 1-hour introduction to numicon programme with follow-up 30 min. lessons supported by TA	All year. May change according to need
	Social skills – small group during registration/tutor time	Group (approx. 6)	1 x 45 mins. per week with TA	All year
	Self-care and independent living skills course	Group (approx. 6)	1 x 45 mins. per fortnight with OTA and/or TA	All year

Individual education plan for student aged 12 years with DCD

Name:	Year:
Date:	Review date:

Target	Strategies	Provision	Success criteria
1. To improve student X's on-task attention in class	To allow student X to select certain pieces of classroom equipment on an as-needed basis to reduce auditory and visual overload	Privacy boards, ear defenders, angled writing board, Dycem™ matting, Fidgets	Improvements based on a pre- and post-time and motion checklist. TA to record on-task and off-task behaviours every 5 minutes for 1½ hours in morning and afternoon, each term Increase on-task behaviours from 5 to 10 within 1 term 10 to 14 within 2 terms 14 to 18 within 3 terms
2. To improve student X's ability to remain seated for the duration of the lesson	Allow student X to sit on either a core disc cushion or a Movin' Sit cushion Note: if possible have 2 of these in use in the classroom so that student X does not feel stigmatised by being the only one to use this equipment	Movin' Sit cushion or core disc cushion Silent electronic timer with visual prompt when 10 minutes have been achieved	Silent electronic timer with visual prompt when 10 minutes have been achieved Full co-operation should be achieved within 1 school term
3. To provide student X with a constructive method of informing their teacher that their tolerance to auditory and visual input is being stretched	Allow student X a subtle method of stating whether the class is too noisy or distracting using a traffic light system: green = tolerance is OK; amber = it is getting hard to concentrate in class; red (red card) = I am struggling to cope with the atmosphere and need a break Alternatively consider their 'engine speed' Note that this could be used for all students rather than student X alone	Traffic prisms or pencil case Refer to the Alert programme for self-modulation	Evaluate whether student X can use such a method for stating their sensory tolerance levels by recording antecedent and subsequent behaviours following the use of this approach This approach will ultimately enable student X to monitor and alter their own stress levels. This should be achieved within 2 school terms Evaluate whether student X can assess their own arousal levels
4. To increase fine motor skills in relation to dressing/undressing prior to and following PE	Subtle adaptation of clothing	An example of how clothing could be adapted will be given to X's parents	Strategies for adapting clothing will be given to student X's parents by week 3 The expectation is that their parents will take responsibility for adapting the school uniform or request assistance in doing this for them

5. To develop student X's handwriting so that they are able to write legibly and at reasonable speed	Small-group *Speed-Up!* kinaesthetic approach to handwriting Assessment of ergonomic tools to improve writing grip and pressure Angle the work so that the wrist is forced to rest on the paper adding stability to their writing	*Speed-Up!* (Addy 2004) Consider the use of a Yoro pen, S'move, and weighted pens to help increase pressure through the writing instrument Introduce the consistent use of an angled writing board	To increase writing speed and legibility from 10 w.p.m. to 18 w.p.m. within 8 weeks
6. To teach word-processing skills	Allow student X to word process homework Allow student X to have dedicated use of a laptop. Teach the use of predictive software	Access to laptop or keyboard Word-processing programme such as TICKEN	Increase typing speed as follows:: Familiar rhyme (repeating a nursery rhyme) from 25 w.p.m. to 35 w.p.m. Cognition (subject given, such as 'All about me') from 20 w.p.m. to 30 w.p.m. by the end of 2 terms
7. To provide alternative methods of written communication	Allow student X to present selected homework via Dictaphone or DVD	Access to a video recorder Access to a Dictaphone	For student X to present 50% of homework using a recording method other than writing.
8. To increase social interaction and social skills	Identify a series of buddies who can be effective role models Introduce student X to 45 min. lunchtime social skills group with the focus on: • volume control • personal space • initiating conversation • listening	Gamesters Handbook Action Speaks Louder social skills book BG Steem assessment	Improved scores on self-esteem checklist such as the BG Steem secondary level checklist, following 3 school terms
9. To improve movement skills, strength and stamina	2 x week (30 mins.) personal trainer session (involving peer, TA or PE student)	Circuit and gym equipment	Increased stamina and time using: • rowing machine • step trainer • running machine • recumbent cycle • weights • therapy ball

But when it comes to writing stuff down, well ... it is not written how I said it in my head.

This is why in my recent exams I did bad beyond belief (I did not even finish any of them let alone get the questions I did do, right.)

Coloured overlays
www.thedyslexiashop.co.uk

Ear defenders
www.ldalearning.com

Exam concessions

Under the Special Educational Needs and Disability Discrimination Act (2001) every effort must be made to enable students with learning differences to reach their potential (this encompasses examinations), and concessions should be made where appropriate so that each individual has the opportunity to present or express what they know. Unfortunately permission for these concessions tends to be inconsistent and to differ according to examination board and regional education authority.

Owing to their slower processing time, laborious and/or illegible handwriting, poor organisational skills and, occasionally, difficulty coping with an auditory–sensitive environment, students with DCD should be able to seek adjustments in examinations. On completion of assessment, the following concessions *may* be available to the individual.

Separate room: Students with DCD are often intimidated by examination conditions, especially when they glance across the room and perceive that their peers are writing prolifically without any effort. Anxiety in addition to co-ordination and perceptual processing concerns may reduce output which is already limited by poor writing or word-processing speed. A smaller, quieter environment can go some way in alleviating this stress.

Posture: The position for writing may increase fatigue experienced by students with DCD whose postural stability is poor. An occupational therapist may advise on seating and table height, and may recommend using a Movin' Sit cushion to stabilise the hips (see page 31). An angled board (see page 32) may improve the position of the script, which benefits posture as well as visual acuity.

Coloured overlays: Like students with dyslexia, those with DCD will often experience the blurring of black text against a white background. This will slow down reading. Coloured overlays may alleviate this visual distress.

Selection of type and size of font: Small text in certain fonts can be difficult to read. Visual figure–ground discrimination difficulties may result in print blurring and visual localisation drifting. The examination questions can be presented in a simple font such as Comic Sans and/or enlarged to 14 point font to ease the reading process. Printing text on pastel-coloured paper may also help. In addition, the provision of a reading window may help to filter the written information (see page 36).

Prompt: Those who have difficulties with attention and/or concentration will benefit from a prompt to keep them on task. This may be in the form of a timer device (obviously silent – e.g. an egg timer) or a physical cue from an assistant.

Equipment: Distractibility can also be managed with the provision of a privacy board to reduce visual distraction, together with ear defenders which will reduce irritating auditory distractions.

Extra time: This is the most common concession. It allows slow readers or writers to have up to 25 per cent extra time to complete a paper. However, when assessing students with DCD it is important not to assume that extra time will resolve handwriting problems. Fatigue, caused by low muscle tone, may be a factor in these, and they cannot be helped by offering more time. Writing legibility deteriorates with fatigue, causing assessors more difficulty when marking. It may be beneficial to allow word processing, or to encourage the binge/snack method of writing – that is, write for ten minutes, rest for two minutes, write for ten, and so on.

Scribe (or amanuensis): Occasionally an assistant is provided who will write on the student's behalf. In order to qualify for this help the student has to demonstrate that their writing is illegible or that they write so slowly that their ability to succeed is prejudiced. The scribe (or amanuensis) must write exactly what is said to them, word for word. This obviously cannot take place in an examination hall, and requires a separate room.

Practical helper / TA: An assistant may carry out commands relating to 'house-keeper'-like duties such as carrying pots and utensils. They are not allowed to offer any factual help.

Reader: If a student has a specific reading difficulty or visual impairment, a reader may be appointed. Students with DCD may struggle with the volume of information on the examination page; the page may appear cluttered, blurred and confusing, causing them to panic and misplace essential detail. They may benefit from a reader to read out each question, at a pace they control themselves.

In addition, there are a number of alternatives to writing that may help the student with DCD.

Tape recorder: It may be possible to use a tape recorder instead of writing down answers to questions. Candidates given this concession submit cassette tapes, CD-ROMs or MP3 recordings, rather than written answer sheets.

DVD: Another option is to record answers visually, using a DVD recorder. Students are read the question and then their response is filmed. The student submits a video or DVD for marking.

Use of a word processor: It is often assumed that individuals with DCD will be able to word process faster than they can write. However, this is not always the case. Word processing requires the precise placement of fingers on a keypad, and this precision may be lacking in those with limited dexterity. However, word-processed text is neat and easy to read. Therefore it is wise to obtain an assessment that compares word processing with written output in terms of legibility and words per minute. A reasonable volume of typed text should be produced before a decision is made to allow word processing.

The interplay between environment, task and student

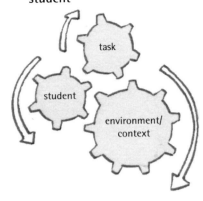

Intervention planning

Assessment without action is a waste of time. Following assessment it is possible to determine whether the difficulties lie in one, two or all areas: the individual, the environment or the task itself. The focus for support is therefore multidimensional.

Individual student: Until recently intervention was focused around changing the individual, the main ethos being to teach the student how to process information and co-ordinate actions in the same way as their peers. It is increasingly evident that this approach is limited, and therefore the wider context needs to be considered.

Interventions that serve to change the developmental course of students with DCD are known as bottom-up or process-orientated approaches. These use carefully taught motor and sensory experiences to help the student integrate information. In helping them to integrate their senses, the premise is that functional skills will improve. For example, if a student is taught to balance on one leg, this will help with functional skills such as stair climbing, athletics, spatial co-ordination, and so on. The focus is on changing the individual.

Task: Sometimes it is the task itself that causes the student stress. The emphasis on handwriting and essays, for example, may have a profound bearing on a student's success. The simple alteration of allowing the student to use a different way to accomplish this task – for instance, word processing – may achieve the objective without any negative impact on self-confidence, effort and self-esteem.

If there is little flexibility in changing the task (i.e. constraints of the curriculum), it is possible to teach the student how to accomplish a task by carefully grading the task itself. This is known as the top-down or task-specific approach. For example, if a student would like to learn to cut a piece of wood, using a fretsaw in a design technology lesson, the task may be carefully graded and introduced to them step by step. The focus is on the task, not the individual.

The environment: Sometimes it is the environment that disables the student. Expecting students to remember facts when the conditions are noisy is not a problem with the student; it is a problem for the student. Because of this, we need to consider the learning environment and context in which our students learn. This is overtly considered in recommendations for examination concessions, but less emphasis is placed on this during day-to-day learning.

A compensatory approach may provide students with adaptive strategies which will help them accommodate their difficulties. Most of the strategies given in this book use this approach.

If I am somewhere where there is lots of people talking then I find my mind gets confused and I can't think properly.

Chapter 4
Practical issues

Survival in secondary education is dependent upon being organised. This involves remembering the correct books/texts, following a timetable, gathering equipment and recalling homework. Most secondary schools house up to two thousand students who are accommodated in countless rooms. Students with DCD will initially struggle to memorise locations, remember directions and organise their routes, especially on occasions when everyone else seems to be moving at the same time. The following practical strategies are recommended to help them.

Helping students to find their way around school

- Location-prompt timetables: Place small pictures on their personal timetable. These should represent significant objects located near the rooms in which the lessons are to take place. They give the student a visible reminder about the location of the room. The objects must have some meaning or be selected by the individual student – examples are a potted plant and a picture of the head teacher.

- Some schools have colour-coded lines (on walls or floor) to aid direction. If these are not provided in your school, they can be suggested.

- Place maps of the school in strategic places around the building, with 'You are here' pointers on them to help students identify their current location. Similar maps are to be found in shopping malls.

- Create a colour-coded timetable with photographs of each teacher the student will come into contact with, and add a symbol or picture prompt for the student to help them with the location of the classroom.

Classroom transfers

Unlike when at primary school, students at secondary level must move to subject-specific classrooms according to their timetable. This may require the student to transfer to up to eight different rooms in one day. This is made more difficult by the fact that the majority of the students will be relocating at the same time. For young people with DCD this may be a traumatic experience as poor spatial planning and co-ordination often leave them feeling claustrophobic when people are pushing and pressing against them in restricted spaces. Noise may be particularly distracting.

In order to cope with crowds, I tend to look down; I also find it helps if I avoid people's eyes. I try to block out as much sensory input as I can, breathing through my mouth instead of my nose, and moving to an area where touching is less likely.

The following ideas are recommended:

- ● Suggest the students take a slightly longer route around school which avoids the majority of crowds.

- ● Give students permission to leave the class a few minutes early so that they can find their next classroom before the rush starts. Please note, however, that there may be a stigma attached to this suggestion.

- ● Suggest that the students use the walls as a reference point so that there is less need for them to adopt the jostles and manoeuvres needed to pass by people.

At the beginning of term this year it was very crowded; I was just about coping with everything and then we got to the main room where they had decided to make things more exciting by having loud music. My brain crashed and took several hours to get back to normal. I completely stopped compensating for my balance and co-ordination, and I lost the ability to talk.

Carrying items

Many secondary schools do not have the space to provide individual lockers. Even when they are provided, students are often required to carry numerous textbooks, together with writing supplies for two to three lessons at a time.

I have excessively poor upper arm strength. I only need to carry two books and a PE kit and my muscles suddenly seize up!

Remembering the correct item is a difficult enough task on its own; carrying heavy items is another problematic matter. Also, the prospect of carrying a tray full of food, together with personal property, in the dining room may be very daunting. At lunch students need to carry their school bags, balance a tray and locate an empty seat in an environment full of noise – and probably strong odours. All this may overwhelm the senses of a student with DCD and be extremely stressful.

The following measures are recommended:

- ● It is possible to buy rucksacks which have small wheels on the base and retractable handles to help propel them along corridors. The use of these will reduce carrying time. These rucksacks could be recommended to parents in the transition information provided prior to commencing secondary school.

- ● Backpacks which have one shoulder strap attached by Velcro at the front are also available. These are easier to put on and off quickly than a standard bag, and with these the weight is distributed evenly across the back and shoulders.

One-strap backpack
www.bagsdirect.co.uk

One-handed tray with non-slip mat

Active Mobility Centre
www.activemobility.co.uk

Retractable key-rings / reels / chains
www.hotfrog.co.uk
www.onestop-key-rings.co.uk

◐ Arrange for students to have two copies of relevant textbooks and to leave one copy in the appropriate classroom. The second is for home use. This minimises the amount that needs to be carried between school and home and around school.

◐ You may suggest that students with DCD will find packed lunches easier to manage than balancing a school meal. However, packed lunches are not always the best choice for growing teenagers. In addition, the social banter of the dining hall may be lost because many schools provide separate facilities for those who bring their own lunch.

◐ Try to allow students with DCD to be part of the first entry into the dining room, so that the chaos of the environment is minimised.

◐ If possible, obtain several one-handed trays with non-slip mats to help students with DCD carry their backpacks together with their lunch.

◐ Allow students who really struggle with sensory modulation issues to eat in a separate classroom. You could also arrange for these students to prepare their own meals in the food technology area.

◐ A meal credit card scheme is frequently used by schools to minimise the need to carry cash. However, these cards are easily lost. If these are used in your school, suggest that the student attaches the card to a retractable chain (available from many suppliers) which may be attached to trousers or an inside jacket pocket

Remembering books and materials

Many young people with DCD have an excellent memory for random facts but need help to remember schedules and homework. Some of the following suggestions are home based and can be discussed with parents/carers in the transition period between primary and secondary school.

◐ Encourage the student to programme the times of lessons and titles of subjects into their mobile phone to prompt them about where they should be and when. They could set a mobile phone alarm (on vibrate mode) to signal key times throughout the day.

◐ Get them to create a visual, colour-coded timetable. Enlarge this to poster size for home use.

◐ Suggest that students collect and pack all relevant textbooks and materials for the day on the previous evening.

◐ If this is feasible, encourage the student to have their own small filing cabinet at home, and to place subject information in separate drawers and label these.

◐ Arrange for a fellow pupil to act as a buddy or mentor, providing the student with a series of prompts each morning.

◐ Encourage the student to obtain a see-through pencil case so that they can easily identify and locate materials they need.

◐ If lockers are available, ensure that the student with DCD is allocated one.

My homework pledges

I will get into the practice of doing my homework
on the day.

I will use a homework diary. I will mark off and sign
each item as soon as it is completed.

I will record homework schedules using a mobile app
such as MyHomework for iPhone and iPad.

I will carry a notebook in my pocket and ask my teachers
to write down what they want me to do.

I will do my homework at school either during the
free time after lunch or (if possible) after school.

Homework

The completion of homework is an essential part of the secondary-school curriculum, and prepares students to be independent learners. In Years 7 and 8 there is an expectation that homework will take 45 to 90 minutes a day; in Year 9, 60 to 120 minutes a day; and in Years 10 and 11, 90 to 150 minutes a day. The main complication lies in the fact that homework in one subject may be given with the expectation that this is completed by three or four days later. Given that up to 14 subjects may be studied simultaneously, confusion can easily arise about what piece of work has to be submitted when.

Personally (I wouldn't recommend this, however) I get by, by writing all important things on my hands. Unfortunately these have a tendency to get smudged, and start creeping up my arms making me look positively tattooed. I try to write in my homework diary, but I can never find it when I need it. I tried to carry it around outside my bag but I kept leaving it in classrooms. I am nowhere near organised enough to keep an appointment diary, I just keep losing it.

Provide a strategy card such as the one opposite: **My homework pledges**.

Staying focused

The noise of someone messing with a plastic bag is what I hate the most.

Students with DCD will have difficulty with maintaining attention and concentrating in the classroom. This is because of the plethora of noises and visual distractions in the room, and the struggles they have in filtering and identifying relevant information. Visual–spatial difficulties may mean that it is difficult for them to locate selected objects visually, especially when these are moving, and/or to allocate sounds to their origin in space. This is not such an issue when didactic teaching takes place – that is, when all students are facing forwards towards the teacher. However, it becomes an issue in subjects such as information technology (IT), DT and art, and in subjects for which furniture is less formally placed, so that the teacher circulates around the classroom.

In addition, poor sensory regulation may cause the student to become restless and fidgety as they crave feedback about where their body is in space. This too may cause them to lose focus. This sensory-seeking behaviour may appear disruptive and annoy others; especially irritating are the habits of rocking their chair backwards and forwards, and stretching their arms as if yawning.

Perceptual difficulties such as poor visual figure–ground discrimination also impact on attention and visual focus. The variety of visual and auditory stimuli within a room may make it difficult to identify a key figure or item on the whiteboard/blackboard. Sudden noises such as an irritating cough or a loud sneeze may be a distraction, causing vital information to be missed.

On a positive note, there is evidence that if the teacher can amplify the focal point in some way (by wearing a brightly coloured jumper or an interesting tie, for instance) the attention of the student with DCD can be improved.

It is for this reason that we need to consider how to modify the learning environment so that not only the students with DCD but all students can sustain attention.

This may be achieved by adopting teaching styles that stimulate the interest and promote the engagement of each student. Students with DCD prefer to learn by **problem-solving** and **physically engaging in the learning process.** Therefore long periods of verbal retort or discussion will be more problematic for them than for others.

The reality is that for the student with DCD attention is a form of endurance athleticism, as running a marathon is for most of us. Training is required to extend potential.

The following strategies may help:

○ Ensure that the student is positioned at the front of the class, facing the teacher. This should help students to obtain a visual focus. But please note the following comment.

Most teachers make me sit at the front ... the only thing is, they also make the students who have misbehaved sit at the front, so as a result I am far more distracted than when I sit with my friends!

○ Encourage the use of a seating plan; this ensures that each student knows where they will sit.

○ Remove excessive materials from the classroom wall immediately behind the teacher, so that visual distractions are minimised.

○ Allow the use of ear plugs / noise-cancelling headphones to filter noise when studying, or for use on an as-needed basis.

I drive my family insane with my wish for silence most of the time. It takes very little noise to distract me from what I'm doing, and much more than that tends to be overwhelming. Large amounts of noise result in my brain refusing to even attempt to process anything, which can be quite distressing.

○ Assess the environment for other potential auditory and visual distractions, such as pictorial displays, noisy heaters, data projector fans and an uneven chair. Adjust these if possible.

I have sensory issues ... for me that lack of filtering happens with auditory, visual, and tactile sensory information. All the info takes on equal importance in my brain. At least for me, it doesn't turn to 'white noise' until right before my brain starts to shut down.

Black print on a stark white background can cause writing to appear blurred. Lines can become confused, and letters seem to b⁰uⁿᶜₑ!

Privacy board
www.ldalearning.com

Movin' Sit cushion
www.ldalearning.com

Core disc cushion
www.tts-group.co.uk

Fidget pencils
www.ldalearning.com

Chewy (oral, motor)
www.sensorydirect.com

- Remind all teachers that when using the interactive whiteboard, the contrast of black print on a shiny stark white background may make letters appear to blur; this is also the experience of students with dyslexia. To counter this, they should reduce the contrast of the whiteboard screen or alter the background to a pastel shade, avoiding the use of red and green colours where possible. They should also be careful about how much information is given at one time and ideally avoid the use of italic fonts and underlining as both may cause confusion.

- Allow the use of privacy boards or learning cordons to reduce visual distractions when studying on an individual basis.

- In order to prevent fidgeting and reduce the risks associated with rocking backwards on a chair, it is important to use a staged approach to increasing vestibular stimulation:

  - Take a soft tennis ball and make a hole in its surface. Place the ball under the base of one leg of the student's chair. This will cause the chair to wobble slightly, which will give vestibular stimulation without the danger of them rocking over backwards.

  - Provide a Movin' Sit cushion. This is an angled soft rubber cushion which has a dimpled surface that is intended to provide sensory feedback to the seated area. The air-filled cushion allows the student to move their hips gently in order to maintain a sense of pelvic stability.

  - A core disc cushion may help instead. Small movements cause sensory feedback that is often lacking in students with DCD. The use of these cushions prevents overt wriggling and avoids the need to stand up.

  - As an alternative a bean-filled cushion can easily be made. This will provide the same results as commercially available air-filled cushions.

  - Finally, it may be necessary to apply a gentle weight through the upper thighs. This can be achieved by providing a weighted lap blanket or encouraging the student to place their bag of files, textbooks and whatever on their laps while they try to concentrate.

- Allow students to manipulate a small object when listening to the teacher. This fidgeting may help the individual to focus. The object can be a piece of Blu-Tack™, a paper clip or an elastic band.

- Encourage the inclusion of movement breaks in lessons to stimulate the student's proprioception.

- Some students with DCD appear to need to move their mouths constantly in order to concentrate. They are craving oral feedback. Students with this issue may chatter incessantly, causing disruption. They may also chew their hair, jumper sleeve or pencil top – indeed, anything vaguely chewable. To alleviate this it is necessary to exercise the oral muscles in a more positive way. Encourage students to have a sports bottle and to drink from it regularly; in addition the use of chewing gum should be supported, although this is typically banned in secondary schools.

Angled writing board
www.ldalearning.com

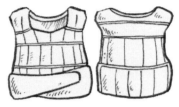

Weighted vest
www.sensorydirect.com
www.rompa.com

◗ Encourage the use of a writing board as this may increase visual focus when writing. These are available commercially, but in secondary school a lever-arch file may suffice instead – although non-slip matting may be an advantage as it will help students to position what they are writing on accurately.

◗ Fluorescent lighting may cause headaches as many students with DCD have scotopic sensitivity. Position these students where natural light is usually available.

◗ Some students benefit from wearing a weighted vest or jacket under their school jumper. This provides deep pressure, calming an overly sensitive tactile system. The jackets are often used for fitness training, but modified versions have been found to be effective with young people whose sensory system is on high alert. The use of these, and the assessment of effective weights, should be discussed with an OT.

Revision for exams

This is a particular concern for students with DCD as the amount of assessment increases in the years leading up to examinations at the ages of 16 and 18 or so, causing anxiety and pressure on the individual. Particular difficulties experienced by students with DCD include inability to organise a revision schedule, writing legibility, reading and absorbing the volume of learning material, and time planning. A list of **Revision hints** for students to use at home (or school) is provided on page 35.

If you are able to provide revision groups at school, encourage students to include the following techniques:

◗ **Mnemonics:** these are rhymes or sentences in which the first letter in each word acts as a prompt to remember routine facts.

   Examples

   ○ To remember the order of geological time periods, the following mnemonic may be used: Cows Often Sit Down Carefully. Perhaps Their Joints Creak? Persistent Early Oiling Might Prevent Painful Rheumatism. (Cambrian, Ordovician, Silurian, Devonian, Carboniferous, Permian, Triassic, Jurassic, Cretaceous, Palaeocene, Eocene, Oligocene, Miocene, Pliocene, Pleistocene, Recent)
   To remember the order of the planets from the sun: My Very Educated Mother Just Served Us Nuts. (Mercury, Venus, Earth, Mars, Jupiter, Saturn, Uranus, Neptune)

   Adding a rap or rhythm to mnemonics may also reinforce learning.

◗ **'Binge and snack' timetable:** this is a realistic timetable in which the study periods (binges) are interspersed with alternative activities (snacks). Some students believe that they have to study for three to four hours at a stretch, but this is often not good practice. A binge and snack timetable may look like this:

Binge and snack timetable

Monday	
8.30	Breakfast
9.00	Binge: practise maths exercises downloaded from the internet
10.00	Snack: watch programme previously recorded on iplayer
10.45	Binge: revise history, identify facts requiring rehearsal and create mnemonics as prompts
12.00	Snack: lunch; during lunch watch two scenes from a Shakespeare DVD
1.00	Binge: revisit experimental procedures undertaken in science, write out key facts. Place unfamiliar words and their definition on Post-It notes and place them on the wall around your bedroom.
2.15	Snack: go for a brief walk, post a letter, etc.
3.00	Binge: focus on chemistry. Rewrite the periodic table of elements, then create a blank test sheet. Test your memory by completing this without any prompts.
4.30	Stop for the day, but first ask family members to test you on your newly written mnemonics.
	Reward yourself for a productive day.

Review how each student's 'binge and snack' timetable is working, discussing any distractions and how to alleviate these.

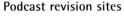

● Use of **DVDs**: many students with DCD are visual learners and therefore will find it easier to remember information by recording it visually rather than through long periods of reading. Try to obtain materials which suit this learning style. Examples are the works of Shakespeare and key texts from English literature on DVD.

● **Mind maps**: teach students how to use mind maps (see example on page 34).

● When **revising languages**, emphasise masculine and feminine nouns by encouraging students to say these out loud: feminine words in a high voice and masculine ones in a deep voice..

Podcast revision sites
www.gcsepod.co.uk
www.bbc.co.uk/schools/gcsebitesize/audio/
www.podcastrevision.co.uk
www.maths-it.org.uk

● **Podcast revision materials**: these can be downloaded to MP3 or iPods. Students can listen to them while having a motor break (a short walk). This has benefits for those who feel guilty when they are not studying directly at a desk. The motor break will improve concentration and attention and therefore expand the student's memory for detail.

● Teach students to draw **diagrams and sketches** that can help them remember points. Wall posters/ charts for visual learners, to remind students of salient GCSE information, are available from www.daydreameducation. co.uk. Pocket posters and revision exercises are also available from this source at a reasonable cost.

I find the only way to remember some things is repetition – normally writing it loads of times. It hurts, but it gets the message through. As with most things, saying it over and over again helps, but can irritate others!

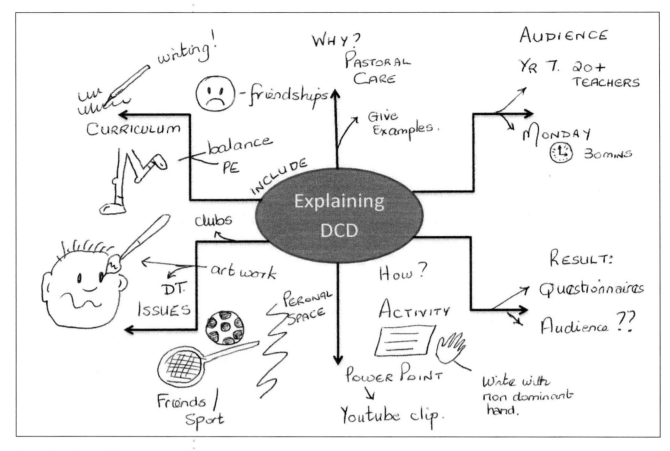

Example of a mind map

MindMapping is the registered trademark of the Buzan Organization.

Flash Revise Pocketbooks
www.hoddereducation.co.uk

○ **Practice papers**: provide the student with opportunities to complete practice papers. Help them to establish a timeframe: break down how much time there is to complete each section and then use a timer to assess how much can be completed in a given time. Set targets for improvement if these are too slow.

> I don't start writing for a while as I have to think through what they are asking. That's probably why I never finish any exams. I always dread the moment where the question says 'Explain'.

○ **Flash cards**: these may be used to rehearse and test knowledge. They include facts and questions and answers on particular subjects. Flash cards can be made or bought. Some commercial flash cards even include notes – for example, Flash Revise Pocketbooks.

Revision hints

- Find a suitable place in your home or school where you are free from distractions. Note that a room where the television can be heard is not conducive to good concentration.

- If you find it difficult to filter out unexpected and varying noises – such as the telephone, the doorbell or voices – use headphones and play some consistent soft music, ideally without lyrics.

- Don't procrastinate. Set a **realistic** objective, write this down and get on with it. If the revision target is too vast, it will quickly become overwhelming and you will probably soon to be despondent.

- Ideally, focus on **understanding** information rather than memorising it, unless the latter is absolutely necessary.

- Work with a study partner, testing each other periodically, alternating reading aloud together, watching DVDs relevant to your topics of study and discussing scenes, and so on.

- Build up a set of study notes for each subject.

- Use **colour** to highlight or underline key points or terms in your written notes.

- Be aware of drink. It will influence concentration levels. Although the caffeine in drinks such as Coca-Cola, Red Bull and Monster may give you an initial boost, the results are short lived and not as effective as drinking water from a sports bottle.

- Remember to watch your diet too. Eating will calm an anxious sensory system. However, what is eaten can affect your concentration. Rather than munching on biscuits, try chewing gum, or crunching on a bowl of vegetables such as peppers, cucumber, celery and carrots.

- Create a 'Binge and Snack' timetable.

- Ensure that you incorporate motor breaks into your day. These will aid your concentration and attention. Do not be tempted to have a break by watching television as there is a risk that you will get absorbed in a programme, which will reduce the time available for you to study.

- COMPUTER ALERT! One of the dangers of revising by using the computer for making notes is the ease in which you can be distracted. It is all very well having good intentions to type notes or colour code information, but the lure of Facebook, My Space, Bebo, Twitter and other social networking sites – as well as an active e-mail account and online games – can lead to your wasting an hour or more. Keep the computer switched off unless you have a specific need to use it.

- SWITCH OFF MOBILE PHONES! Ideally place your phone in another room to help you resist the temptation of answering incoming text messages or phone calls.

The examination

The use of continuous assessment has been recently challenged in favour of two- to three-hour examinations. English children are now the most tested children in the industrialised world, with the average pupil subjected to at least 70 tests during their school career (*Guardian* 2011). Examinations are stressful to most pupils, but particularly so for those with DCD, whose hands tire more quickly with the effort of writing than their peers' do, and whose memory, organisation and planning are often compromised.

Apart from the concessions recommended in Chapter 3, there are a number of strategies that may help the student within the examination itself:

- Provide the student with a colour-coded examination schedule. Include location and time. Give a copy to a mentor/buddy/friend who will provide a prompt, text, e-mail or verbal reminder.
- Provide a quiet room for the student prior to the examination and encourage them not to talk over what they have learned with a peer as the mention of material they have not focused on may cause panic.
- Ensure the invigilator knows of any previously agreed accommodations or concessions – for example, related to time and/or presentation. (Many schools use external invigilators who may not have been party to discussions and may not know the circumstances of individual students.)
- If necessary, arrange for a member of staff to read each question to the student.
- Encourage the student to read all the instructions carefully, using a reading window to filter and enhance relevant information.
- Encourage the use of a highlighter pen to underline key words in the questions.
- Encourage the student to estimate how long each question will take to answer and to write that down on a rough time plan like the one below.

A reading window may be used to highlight pertinent information

Reading window
www.ldalearning.com

Examination time plan

Geography: Paper 1 Time 1½ hours			
Question	Approx.	Start	Finish
Read through	10 minutes	10.00	10.10
1	10 minutes	10.10	10.20
2	15 minutes	10.20	10.35
3	10 minutes	10.35	10.45
4	20 minutes	10.45	11.05
5	10 minutes	11.05	11.15
6	Read through, edit and correct	11.15	11.30

Be sure to encourage the student to include time for planning, writing, proof reading and correcting.

Chapter 5
Curricular issues

Handwriting

It is expected that by Key Stage 3 students will have handwriting that is fast, fluent, legible and neat. The curriculum's direction in relation to handwriting ends at the age of 9, when it is assumed that this complex motor, perceptual and cognitive skill will have been mastered. Unfortunately, students with DCD will continue to experience the stresses of co-ordinating an unruly pen well into their teens, with a consequent effect on self-confidence and self-esteem.

Although it is argued that handwriting is a dated and irrelevant method of recording information, it is worth stressing that the practice of handwriting improves perceptual processes such as form constancy, helps with organisation and planning, and improves manual dexterity. In addition, research highlights the hand's unique relationship with the brain when it comes to composing thoughts and ideas.

National Handwriting Association

www.nha-handwriting.org.uk

When addressing handwriting concerns it is important to consider:

- Ergonomic tools
- Writing posture
- Writing pressure
- Organisation and writing
- Writing speed and legibility
- Fatigue
- Alternatives to handwriting.

Ergonomic tools

Initially it is important to help students experiment with ergonomic tools – pens, pencils and crayons – to assist them in developing an appropriate grip that will help with manipulation, pressure placement, posture and writing flow. It is impossible to prescribe a pen/pencil that will initiate perfect legibility. However, the following have proved useful:

- The Yoropen™ and Yoropencil™. These are also available as pencil crayons and therefore may be used in art.

- The PenAgain™ which aligns the index finger directly to the pen point, subsequently enhancing writing control.

- The S'move™ pen and S'move™ pencil are available in left- and right-hand versions. These are available from many suppliers and also in supermarkets.

- A Ring pen is particularly useful for positioning, preventing the writing instrument from slipping into the incorrect position.

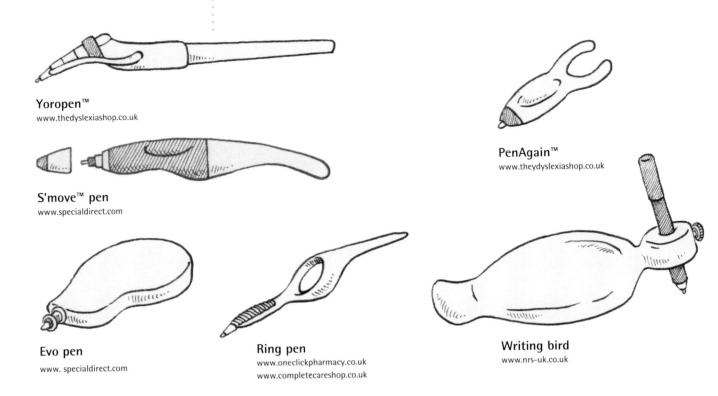

Yoropen™
www.thedyslexiashop.co.uk

S'move™ **pen**
www.specialdirect.com

Evo pen
www. specialdirect.com

Ring pen
www.oneclickpharmacy.co.uk
www.completecareshop.co.uk

PenAgain™
www.theydyslexiashop.co.uk

Writing bird
www.nrs–uk.co.uk

- An Evo pen forces the hand to develop an accurate tripod grip.
- A writing bird glides over the page with minimal effort. It enables the student to control the pen without being concerned about the pressure through the writing tool.

Writing posture

One of the dilemmas in a large secondary school is the diverse array of classrooms. Unlike in primary school, it is likely to be very difficult to allocate classroom furniture to an individual student. Ideally the writing posture should be adapted for the student, so their feet are flat on the floor, knees are at 90°, and the height of the table is parallel to arms bent to 90°.

When the table is too high or too low, pressure through the writing tool becomes erratic and motor control is impaired.

There are a number of practical adjustments that will help students develop the optimum working position:

- Provide a wooden block or a thick catalogue. One can be located in each relevant classroom. It should be slipped under the table to serve as a foot block to provide the student with a secure base from which to work.
- Provide a thick square cushion in each classroom. It is may be used to raise the seat height to accommodate tall students.
- Encourage the use of an A4 lever-arch file to angle the paper position in order to optimise writing posture.
- Encourage students to carry a Posture Pack™ (www.backinaction.co.uk) that includes items they need to assist them in attaining an optimal position.

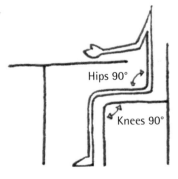

Hips 90°

Knees 90°

Table too low

Table too high

Kneeling chair in use
www.backinaction.co.uk
www.sitkneelchairs.co.uk

Light-Up pen
www.ldalearning.com
www.thedyslexiashop.co.uk

MI5 carbonated pad
www.specialdirect.com

Weighted cuff or wrist weight
www.therapyshoppe.com

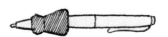

Weighted pen
www.wessexhealthcare.co.uk
www.disability-warehouse.co.uk

Pen/pencil weights
www.kidmart.co.uk
www.welcomemobility.co.uk

◐ **A kneeling-chair** may be needed in some classrooms. These chairs force the muscles of the trunk to work hard to maintain an upright posture. This provides both an accurate seating position and simultaneous exercise. As the chair provides proprioceptive feedback through the knees, buttocks and spine, the tendency to wriggle is lessened.

Writing pressure

The amount of pressure placed through a pen or pencil will either free or limit writing speed and flow. Students who are compelled to write at speed will increasingly tense their muscles, causing them to increase the downward pressure through the writing instrument. This may hinder fluency. Sometimes, students with DCD are unable to adjust the pressure placed through their arm when writing owing to poor proprioceptive feedback and need a weighted aid.

The following may help with either too much or too little pressure:

◐ Encourage the student to use a pressure-activated light-up pen. When the light comes on, this signals heavy pressure. The indicator enables the student to learn by self-regulation.

◐ Encourage the student to write revision notes, homework notes, and so on using a carbonated writing pad (or MI5™ pad). Explain that they should attempt to adjust the pressure so that the notes are legible only on one layer of paper. If the student's writing pressure is too light the opposite may help: they should practise writing notes that appear on more than one sheet of carbonated paper.

◐ Providing a weighted wrist band or forearm cuff will give feedback through the forearm muscles, which should improve control and pressure for students with poor proprioceptive feedback. These devices can be hidden under a school jumper.

◐ Alternatively it is possible to weight the writing instrument itself by adding weights. You can also buy specially weighted pens.

Teachers need to be aware that students with DCD may be struggling with grammar and spelling. This may not have been picked up during the primary years. When students have difficulty with spelling they tend to press down more heavily than usual, and they will write over words and smudge words that they perceive to be spelt incorrectly. At this stage it is important to identify specific difficulties. The following are examples:

○ omissions (missed letters);

○ substitutions (wrong letters);

○ insertions (superfluous letters);

○ reversals.

Dyslexia screening may be needed to make sure that appropriate support is given.

Right-Line® paper
www.thedyslexiashop.co.uk

Raised line paper
www.livingmadeeasy.org.uk

Embossed graph paper
www.rnib.org.uk

Label Me!
www.enchantedlearning.com

Organisation and writing

Students with DCD struggle with organisation. This has an impact when they are attempting to organise a page of composition or columns of numbers. Spatial difficulties affect word alignment, where to commence and when to move to a new line. There are a number of strategies that may be taught to help the student in this situation:

○ Provide lined paper with a different coloured margin for these students. Encourage them to start each line at the left-hand margin.

○ If a coloured line does not provide the student with a clear enough reference point, introduce paper that includes a kinaesthetic prompt – for example, raised-line paper such as Right-Line® paper.

○ Grid paper may be used – especially for mathematics, where the correct placement of numbers in columns is essential.

○ When students are asked to label a diagram, rather than expecting them to attempt to create a line to the desired point and write in a confined area, encourage them to use coloured narrow labels. Suggest that they look at the diagram and write each term on a separate sticker before peeling these off and placing them next to the relevant item.

○ Encourage the use of printed-out labels rather than getting students to attempt to draw diagrams and label them.

Writing speed and legibility

By the time the student has reached secondary school they will have been writing for seven years. It is very difficult to change a repeatedly used, consistently practised ineffective writing style after all this time. This does not mean that handwriting tuition has no place, but a different approach may be necessary.

My bad handwriting has gotten me into trouble on many occasions. I either have acceptable handwriting, or acceptable pace, never both.

Often it is the speed and legibility of handwriting that is the major issue at this age. The absence of effective feedback through the muscles makes it harder for the student with DCD to determine how much pressure to apply, affecting the automaticity of writing. There are three approaches to handwriting that may be used at this stage: multisensory, cognitive-behavioural, and rehearsal.

Multisensory approach: We know that many students with DCD struggle with sensory and kinaesthetic processing (that is, the sense of movement and awareness of the position of the limbs that arise from information from the joints, muscles and tendons). Complex fine motor skills such as handwriting require high-level processing and kinaesthetic memory, which helps to regulate pressure through the limbs and monitor patterns of movement. Students who lack sensory feedback quickly learn how to compensate for this by using other sensory cues, in particular vision (which is the strongest sense). This compensation unfortunately slows down the speed of handwriting.

Loops and Other Groups:
A Kinesthetic Writing System
www.pearsonassessments.com

Callirobics (advanced and adults'
editions)
www.specialdirect.com

To address this there are several multisensory handwriting programmes which aim to stimulate the motor, kinaesthetic and tactile senses and in doing so improve the speed and fluency of handwriting production. These include *Loops and other Groups* by Mary Benbow (1999); *Callirobics* by Liora Laufer (1990) and *Speed-Up!* by Lois Addy (2004).

These programmes incorporate a variety of strategies such as vibration, resisted writing and writing on a blackboard (both horizontal and against a wall); motor learning techniques such as shaping, grading and letter formation; and behavioural approaches involving goal setting and fading. All these help to develop writing alignment, spacing and letter sizes.

The aim of the programmes is to stimulate the senses using exercises, games and a variety of multisensory activities to enhance the motor memory required to obtain fast, fluent handwriting. Concentrated input provides the stimulation needed.

Speed-Up! A kinaesthetic programme
to develop fluent handwriting
www.ldalearning.com

For example, *Speed-Up!* is an intensive 8-week kinaesthetic handwriting programme for children aged between 3 and 8 years. It involves a one-hour tutorial each week and regular daily rehearsal. Used by teachers or therapists, it usually involves a small group of students. Initially students are introduced to a series of carefully selected physical exercises that take approximately ten minutes to complete. These serve to increase shoulder and hip girdle stability while stimulating the proprioceptors of the upper limbs. These activities are incorporated into a daily regime and particularly before handwriting activities.

Speed Up! Blackboard
www.ldalearning.com

Speed-Up! incorporates the use of a double-sided blackboard to encourage bilateral hand skills and enhance the motor memory by vibrating the muscles. The vibrations produced by the friction of chalk against the surface stimulate upper limb kinaesthetic sense while increasing stability at the shoulder girdle. Much of the programme involves non-visual activities relating to handwriting, and it is only during the latter stages that vision and speed writing are introduced. Results from this programme have been generally positive.

Samples of handwriting
before and after following
the *Speed-Up!* kinaesthetic
writing programme.

Pre-programme

Post-programme

> Kevin Vladd was not looking forwards to Tuesday evening His parents, Mr and Mrs Vladd, were not looking forwards to Tuesday evening. And his teacher Mrs Fottle, was not looking forwards

> do if they were hungry but there was nothing he could do about it. The classroom door opened and Grant and his mum came out Grant stuck out his tongue Kevin looked away. He went into the classroom with his parents, "Kevin's maths has got better," Mrs Fottle began, "

Cognitive-behavioural approach: This approach is particularly good for motivated students who are determined to improve their handwriting legibility and speed. It is often referred to as a self-instructional training model or consultative clinical reasoning process as it encourages students to self-evaluate their handwriting and identify how they could improve output. It involves the use of modelling, imitation, discussion, guided practice and self-evaluation.

The principles of this approach are based on Vygotsky's understanding of private speech: young children often solve problems by talking out loud to themselves but as they become older this talk becomes internalised. This vocal self-instruction can help students to express their problem-solving ability while allowing the teacher to understand how they process information, offering guidance when appropriate. Six stages may be identified in this approach:

1 the adult models the task while talking out loud (cognitive modelling);
2 the student performs the task while the adult provides instructions out loud (overt, external guidance);
3 the student performs the task while verbalising instructions (overt self-guidance);
4 the student is encouraged to identify any difficulties – such as legibility – and find a solution to these;
5 the student performs the task while whispering instructions (faded, overt-self-guidance);
6 gradually the student performs the task using private speech (covert self-instruction).

The results of this approach are good, but do require 1:1 tuition. There is also a concern that its transferability to writing tasks outside the tutorial session may be limited.

Rehearsal approach: A further method, known as the social-cognitive approach, also involves the teacher/therapist modelling and providing guided practice. Establishing specific tasks and independent practice are key to improving legibility and skill. This method also encourages self-instruction and advises the students to establish goals using easily measured criteria such as time and letter legibility. For example, the target may be set to write 20 words of three or more letters a minute. These need to be written legibly. Words that cannot be read (out of context) are discounted.

Alternatively more formal assessments can be used to measure speed and legibility and provide a more objective target. The Detailed Assessment of Speed of Handwriting (DASH; Barnett *et al.* 2007) is a comprehensive test, and recently an assessment for those who are 17 and over has been added.

Fatigue

One of the dilemmas of writing in secondary school is the volume required, and another is the pressure of time. Writing may involve copying from a whiteboard, blackboard or text, or taking dictation. Not only do students with DCD struggle with legibility and speed, but they will also tire more quickly than their peers. Fatigue has a significant effect on handwriting speed, letter formation, spatial organisation and ergonomics. Research has shown that when students were asked to write long texts, fatigue had a significant effect on their handwriting, owing to increasingly poor posture, muscle cramps, distorted spatial organisation and increased pencil pressure. It is therefore important that strategies are provided to reduce this pressure:

- Encourage students to use shorthand when note-taking. It is possible to learn a formal system of shorthand or to use a simple modified system such as writing the initial three letters of each word, leaving space after each to enable returning to fill in the words later as shown below.

tdy it is vry w and r y
I w t to go to the sh b
I th k it m y b too w t.

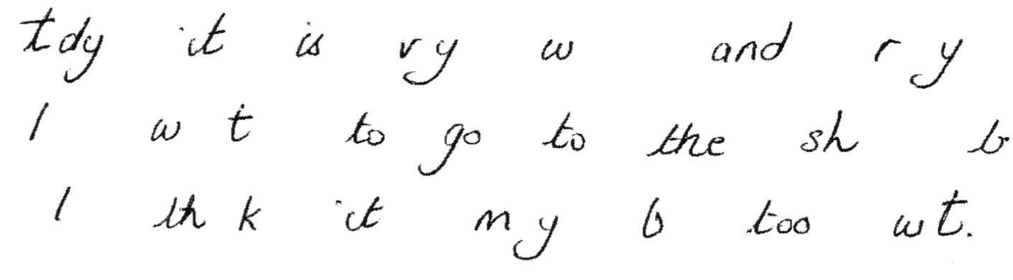

- Reduce the need for students to copy from textbooks by providing them with a print-out of the work required (this is a concession allowed in most universities, so it should be available to secondary-school students).
- Keep a range of ergonomic pens and pencils. When using these the position of the writing tool can be altered to improve comfort when the student's hand tires (see page 38 for examples).
- Encourage the student to improve their posture and writing position by tilting work upwards using an angled writing board (see page 32). When using this equipment the posture remains upright, which will improve spatial planning and optimise upper muscle strength.
- Encourage students to build in motor breaks when working. In these breaks the hands can be rubbed, massaged and stretched. In exams this kind of break could be inserted between test questions.

Detailed Assessment of Speed of Handwriting (DASH)
www.pearsonclinical.co.uk

Modified shorthand; full words may be filled in later

Angled writing board
www.ldalearning.com

○ Try to limit the volume of work which is visible to the student. Students with DCD tend to panic if they are aware, for example, that a large sheet of writing is to be copied. This will lead to increased muscle tension, and subsequently to fatigue. Get them to cover work with a plain sheet of paper so that paragraphs are revealed one at a time.

○ Encourage the use of symbols to help with note-taking.
For example, @ = at, Rx = treatment, ∴ = therefore.
They can create their own personal symbols as appropriate.

○ Allow the student to write in text speak (e.g. @TEOTD = at the end of the day). Remind them that they must convert this usage to acceptable grammar before any formal submission of work.

○ Allow the student to use a Dictaphone to record information, with the class teacher's permission, of course.

Alternatives to handwriting

Thankfully, many schools now allow young people to word process pieces of work, including homework. It is also a useful alternative when legibility begins to affect grades. However, word processing is not necessarily an easier or more appropriate option for those whose fine motor co-ordination and spatial planning lack precision. It is therefore important to assess the benefits of writing over typing before a decision is made.

Consider the following questions:

○ Can the student isolate their index fingers?

○ Can the student locate the letters on the keyboard?

○ Is the pressure placed on each key appropriate or too heavy / too light?

○ Does the student struggle to transfer visually from screen to keyboard?

If the answer to most or all of these is negative, it may be preferable to continue with handwriting as the main form of written communication.

Many programmes are available for learning to type. The website given here may help with choosing a suitable one.

Should poor fine motor skills limit the speed of word processing, it may be appropriate to consider introducing a voice-activated programme such as Dragon Naturally Speaking Premium or J-Say Pro. Be aware that these are not necessarily easier options as training is needed for the computer to recognise speech patterns, which may be problematic when a student's voice is breaking. Also, a computer will not ensure that typing is grammatically correct, and misinterpretation is common. For example 'youth in Asia' could appear as 'euthanasia', and vice versa.

Another method of helping students to attain legible script is to use writing-to-type devices such as scanning pens, digiscribble pads and the Livescribe's Echo Smartpen Starter Pack and apps such as WritePad by Apple.

Typing advice:
www.superkids.com/aweb/pages/reviews/typing/

Guidance on hardware:
www.AbilityNet.co.uk

J-Say Pro
www.astec-at.co.uk

Scanning Pen
www.scanningpens.co.uk

Apcom Digiscribble Mobile Digital Pen
www.invate.co.uk

Livescribe Echo Smartpen
www.pcworld.co.uk

Sport and physical education

Secondary PE may be particularly problematic for students with DCD. At this stage of education, team sports are encouraged and sporting prowess gives status and popularity, especially among boys. This is easily the subject in which students with DCD are most vulnerable and where their self-esteem is most easily quashed. Team selection and competition provide added pressure on speed, agility, complex spatial planning and peer pressure. For many students with DCD, avoidance strategies such as forgetting their PE kit, feigning sickness, absenteeism, sabotage and even truancy are not uncommon.

I hate PE. I try every excuse in the book! I managed to get my teacher to believe I had a disorder that means I have to sleep if I get tired! ... I 'suddenly' get tired every PE lesson or I go to the school nurse. I manage to give a different excuse every lesson! In the end they gave up on trying to make me do it!

There is evidence that students with DCD constantly constrain or limit their movements in order to balance, assess space visually, cope with unexpected jostles, plan an activity and so on. This affects their fluency, speed and freedom of movement, making them look clumsy. It is therefore important that when new tasks are introduced or physical skills are expanded to encompass team games, these are practised in a number of situations. Variables such as the floor surface, sounds, smells and other participants have to be taken into consideration, so that students can learn how to generalise their skills in a selection of settings. For example, it is possible to teach a student with DCD how to kick a football into a goal placed ten metres away in a school sports hall, but can the same student achieve this on a playing field? In the school yard? While wearing shoes, not trainers? If the weather is cold? If there are other participants? The variables interact to make our body a dynamic system. This is an important aspect of motor learning as students' long-term motor proficiency and engagement in physical activity will be shaped by their experiences of physical education while at school.

Despite having difficulties in many sporting activities, there are certain sports which students with DCD may become exceptionally good at. With determination and encouragement they may become highly proficient in many solo or small team sports such as running, martial arts, rowing and horse riding. Also, many secondary schools have equipment that is not available in primary schools which encourages fitness and health. Examples are swimming pools and fully equipped gyms.

I was absolutely hopeless at all sports until I discovered athletics; my teacher taught me how to run in a straight line. I practised looking at an end point and running towards it as fast as I could. With practice I got faster and faster. My teacher once tried to introduce hurdles but that was impossible, I couldn't work out the height or distance to the hurdle and fell flat on my face! I think I'll stick to the 100-metre run and save my knees!

Here are some strategies to help students who have difficulty in sport and PE:

○ Students with DCD are at risk of becoming obese because they tend to be sedentary, so encourage them to focus on the development of physical skills rather than on competitive team sports. Support each student in setting personal goals and then aiming to break their personal best.

○ In order to help the student learn about spatial organisation, distances and speed of movement, try to keep the learning environment as predictable as possible. This will help them to learn and practise in a consistent environment before trying more complex activities.

○ Sports involving ball skills or the manipulation of objects are often more difficult for students with DCD. Consider introducing sports where spatial planning and movement may be restricted, such as volleyball, hockey, fencing and judo. Other possibilities are those in which the object may be graded in terms of speed. For instance, in badminton the shuttlecock is passed at a slower speed than that of a tennis ball (depending on who is hitting the shuttlecock, of course).

○ Try to encourage proficiency in lifestyle sports such as golf, climbing, circuit training, dance, rowing, cycling, martial arts, yoga and swimming. Students with DCD should always wear safety gear when cycling as they are at greater risk of falling or knocking into people and objects.

○ Emphasise fun and participation rather than achievement.

○ Break down activities into smaller parts and encourage the individual to practise skills in an unpressurised environment or small group before they join in whole-class PE lessons. The titles of extra-curricular groups should be carefully chosen to motivate students to attend, so you might ask them to participate in a physical literacy programme or advanced PE module.

○ Use a cognitive-behavioural approach to encourage each student to consider what they are doing, and to analyse and amend their own performance. For example, analyse individual actions and ask such questions as 'Do you need to kick the ball harder or not quite so hard?'

○ If a student is interested in a sport, even if they can't play it well, their interest should be encouraged. They might, for instance, become an expert on players and teams, which would help them to maintain their street cred.

○ If students are required to have some involvement in competitive sports, encourage the PE teacher to choose the teams, especially if there is any risk of the individual being the last to be picked or, worse, ignored.

○ When sports and games which are new are being introduced, provide the student with a copy of the rules in advance so that they have the opportunity to familiarise themselves with the tasks required, positions and expectations of participants.

○ A student whose DCD causes problems with moving and listening simultaneously will find fast-action games such as netball, rugby or football very difficult as many skills are needed at one time. Do not put the student in a position where the success of the game will depend on their skills – for example, goalkeeper or centre forward. Have high aspirations and praise effort without being condescending or patronising.

I love swimming, it's the only sport I don't find a huge struggle.

◗ It is possible to adapt or differentiate class-based activities to ensure that the student is successful. There are four ways in which this may be achieved:

   ○ The environment can be adapted – for instance, the court's size can be reduced when playing hockey, volleyball or badminton.

   ○ The equipment can be adapted – for example, provide a short-handled racquet for tennis, lower the net, and introduce a batting tee.

   ○ The rules can be altered – for example, there can be fewer players in each team, and the ball can be bounced.

   ○ The game may be altered fundamentally – for example, you can devise floor versions of lacrosse or football, and volleyball may be played seated.

Overall it is vital that the student finds an area of PE that is stimulating and motivating for them, and in which they are able to achieve a measure of success. The attitude and understanding shown by the PE teacher at this stage may well be instrumental in promoting an active and healthy lifestyle. On the other hand, they may lead to the student adopting a sedentary lifestyle in which they avoid activity because of fear of humiliation and embarrassment.

Short-handled tennis racquet
www.sportsequipmentsupplies.com

Up Rite Safe Tee
www.daviessports.co.uk

My co-ordination is terrible and the teacher always has a go at me, saying 'You live in your own world, you have a zone where you convince yourself that you can't do anything and so you don't try.'

I say, 'Well, I can't do it.'

She says, 'No, you just don't try.'

I ignore her generally, but sometimes she threatens to give me one-to-one lessons at lunch times. That annoys me. I can't catch very well at all, can't hit the ball with the softball bat either. I don't really want to spend another 40 minutes each day on that!

Art and design technology

The subjects that are most problematic for pupils with DCD at primary school are those involving writing, PE and art. It is in these areas that difficulties in fine motor and perceptual skills are amplified, and this has a profound effect on self-esteem and self-confidence. With regard to the creative arts, at secondary school a variety of activities is included, ranging from traditional art to sculpture, technical drawing, design, dance and drama. While traditional art remains difficult for many students with DCD, they have the ability to excel in other creative subjects. In fact their quirkiness and unusual resourcefulness give them advantages and their achievements in some of the activities included in these subjects may be applauded.

It does take me a very long time to draw. I failed art at school because I could not draw anything good in the time limit, because when I have to draw fast my pictures are very, very bad.

It is evident when we analyse the task of drawing that, like handwriting, it is a very complex activity that takes a lot of time and energy. When drawing from life a student has to observe an object very carefully and obtain a visual memory of it. Before being able to draw it they must learn the conventions of the two-dimensional medium, such as depth perception, perspective, size

Art support
http://www.allaboutdrawings.com/draw-by-tracing.html
http://drawright.com/vaceface.htm

and shape, and spatial organisation. They then have to recall the appropriate information, just as they recall the relevant information when copying script from a blackboard or whiteboard. The short-term memory problems experienced by many students with DCD render this problematic. They need to be able to take a three-dimensional object or scene and flatten it on a sheet of paper. In most art curricula, cognitive modelling (drawing and model making) is central to art and design activity. It is therefore important to address the significant issues experienced and provide strategies to support the student practically.

Different areas of the brain are engaged when drawing from imagination from those involved in drawing from life. Drawing from the imagination involves proportion, orientation and spatial organisation in order to establish effective perimeters and scale.

Swansea Institute, Dynevor Centre for Art, Design & Media,
Swansea, SA1 3EU
http://www.saatchi-gallery.co.uk/artcolleges/ArtCollege/Swansea+Institute+/60.html

A verbal–cognitive approach has been found to be helpful with these issues at the Swansea Institute Faculty of Art and Design. Researchers created opportunities for students to draw both from life and from imagination, under the guidance of a set of instructions. These are summarised as follows:

◗ Focus attention. Consider the tactics recommended in Chapter 4, **Staying focused**, pages 29–32.
◗ Give a general overview of what is expected.
◗ Introduce and explain new terms such as proportion, dimension, depth, analysing, designing, competence, artefacts and culture.
◗ Go through any new procedure step by step.
◗ Model the process: think aloud and introduce new frameworks of thought. Students can also discuss the process and techniques with each other. The use of verbalisation and interactive discussion helps them to clarify and to organise and order mentally what is expected from them.
◗ Guide the practice – get the students to repeat the instructor's strategy with support.
◗ Provide opportunities for independent practice.
◗ Redemonstrate the practice, if necessary, to reinforce the process.

In spite of everything I shall rise again: I will take up my pencil, which I have forsaken in my great discouragement, and I will go on with my drawing.

Vincent Van Gogh

Creative Mentors Foundation
www.creativementors.co.uk

In addition, the following techniques recommended by the Creative Mentors Foundation are very helpful:

◗ Tracing is a tool that may be used to improve freehand drawing. It helps the student to visualise what they are drawing and reinforces the motor memory so that they effectively see the image and physically repeat it. However, it is important to encourage students to stick both the image to be traced and the tracing paper down on a table so that they do not slip, and effort is focused on the image rather than on struggling to hold the paper in position.

Graph and grid paper PDFs
www.incompetech.com

◗ Use a grid; it may help with spatial planning, size and proportion. This is not a form of cheating. Great artists such as Leonardo da Vinci used this approach. Use a computer grid generator to section the picture prior to its reproduction. There are several practice sheets available to download.

Perspective (drawing)
www.olejarz.com

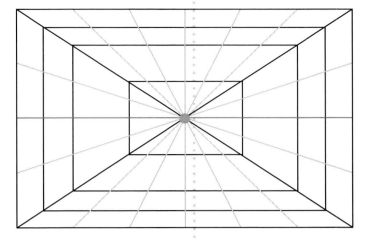

❍ Use a perspective frame such as the one shown below. This may help to develop proportion and depth awareness.

❍ Negative space drawing. This is a technique in which the student concentrates on drawing the empty space around an object rather than the object itself.

Easy grip scissors
www.hope-education.co.uk

❍ Drawing with scissors. Henri Matisse used scissors as a drawing tool. He said, 'The paper cut-out allows me to draw in the colour … Instead of drawing the outline and putting the colour inside it … I draw straight into the colour.' Matisse tore shapes too. Students with DCD may try combining cut and torn shapes. The scissors used can be spring-assisted or push-down / desk-based to assist with co-ordination.

❍ Cartooning. This involves amplifying and exaggerating aspects of your subject. Inaccuracies in proportion and form may enhance images.

Spring-assisted scissors
www.hope-education.co.uk

Although still-life drawings and paintings are especially difficult for students with DCD, this should not deter them from expressing their creativity. They could use abstract designs and alternative methods such as mosaic, collage, decoupage, papier-mâché, clay, acrylics, and felting and other structured materials.

Mathematics

Many students with DCD have difficulty with mathematics. For some this will be due to poor organisation, spatial planning and other perceptual deficits; for others to poor short-term memory problems. Still others may have a discrete mathematical disability known as **dyscalculia**, a condition that affects the ability to acquire arithmetical skills. The latter group will have difficulty understanding simple number concepts, lack an intuitive grasp of numbers, and have problems learning number facts and procedures.

> I have really bad problems with maths. I get numbers muddled up, flip them upside down, and see them backwards. I also have difficulty actually applying mathematical concepts (for instance, I sometimes add when I should divide or forget all the procedures).

The perceptual difficulties experienced by most students with DCD will influence their ability to arrange the page, and to create appropriate columns and rows. That may leave teachers puzzled about how they processed the information in the first place. Students will have trouble with directionality, struggling to discriminate between left and right. They may also have a tendency to reverse or mistype numbers and symbols, and to misplace decimal points. There will be particular problems with geometry owing to their having to use such equipment as a compass or protractor, and with activities involving spatial planning (e.g. drawing shapes, graphs and tables). Angles and diagonals are especially problematic as they cross two planes: top to bottom and left to right.

> My maths teacher isn't quite sure what to do with me!
>
> My numerical skills are good but when it comes to shape, coordinates and symmetry...oh dear!

Short-term memory problems may also have an impact on the multistage processes involved in many calculations. On a positive note, long-term memory is seldom impaired, so with considerable practice facts can be acquired and recalled.

The following strategies may be helpful:

- Encourage the student to carry a cue card as an aide-memoire to help them recall selected formulae.
- Ask the student to apply the calculation to a real-life scenario or problem in order to 'ground' the information – otherwise it may seem somewhat abstract and arbitrary. For example, ask 'If your aim is to buy a car that costs £2,535 and you get £5 per week pocket money, and on average £45 for your Christmas and birthday presents, how long will it take you to save up for the car?'
- Suggest that the student may wish to purchase a watch which has both the 24-hour digital and analogue times displayed.
- Encourage multisensory approaches as much as possible. The more practical maths, the better.
- Encourage the student to try to visualise mathematical problems.

Tinted-grid exercise books
www.thedyslexiashop.co.uk

At the moment in maths we are learning how to measure angles, using a protractor.

I find this part of maths especially difficult. Today someone gave me a round-wheel protractor with an arrow thing on it. I found this slightly easier but when I used it I kept wobbling and losing the position.

Large-print flexible ruler
www.hope-education.co.uk

Talking calculators,
big-number calculators, folding
geometric shapes
www.rnib.org.uk

Fraction shapes
www.rnib.org.uk

- ◑ Introduce graph paper to help with page organisation. If possible, provide raised-line graph paper.

- ◑ Introduce tinted-grid exercise books to help students visualise the problems more clearly and aid page organisation.

- ◑ Encourage the student to learn estimation techniques using something solid such as body parts, size of step, time and speed. For example, 'My fingernail measures approximately 1 cm; from the tip of my thumb to the knuckle is about 3 cm.'

- ◑ Introduce practical measurement tools such as Cuisenaire rods, Base Ten Dienes blocks and Fraction Towers to accommodate spatial and visual closure difficulties. All of these are widely available.

- ◑ Encourage the student to place a small blob of Blu-Tack on each end of a ruler and on the back of a protractor to stop these slipping when attempting measuring tasks or calculating angles.

- ◑ Basic concepts such as horizontal, vertical, rows, columns, perpendicular, diagonal, parallel, intersecting and steeper may have to be taught, and practised regularly. These can be reiterated by connecting them to objects, for instance by pointing out that pages in a book and most swimming pools are rectangular; plates and CDs are circular; Beyblades are hexagonal, and so on.

- ◑ Rather than risking their becoming overwhelmed by trying to read and calculate written problems/calculations at the same time, read out sums for the student at a careful pace. Alternatively it may be possible to record mathematical problems on to an MP3 player.

- ◑ Sometimes attempting to read the minuscule numbers on a ruler is too difficult; a large-print flexible ruler (tape measure) may help.

- ◑ Invest in a talking calculator with ear phones. This is a desktop calculator that performs standard mathematical functions and percentages and recalls the numbers programmed. It may help the student to determine whether the correct number has been inserted – a calculation will go wrong, often seriously, if even one number has been inserted incorrectly.

- ◑ Consider obtaining a big-number calculator. This is a desktop calculator with large clear keys and display that performs standard mathematical functions and percentages. It should help with spatial organisation.

- ◑ It is possible to purchase folding geometric shapes. These may help in the creation of three-dimensional nets, which are particularly useful for teaching area, surface area, symmetry, perimeter, shape, angles and volume.

- ◑ Introduce geoboards so that students can create shapes in order to learn about angles, rotation, scaling, patterns and perimeters.

- ◑ There are several practical tools that may help students to appreciate fractions. For example, plastic fraction shapes, such as ones which combine to form whole circles, and Fraction Towers.

- ◑ It may be better to use a combination of description and a two-dimensional diagram, and work with the solid shape, rather than using three-dimensional diagrams. For example, when setting an exercise relating to prisms, you

Moziblox Mosaic Cubes
www.moziblox.com

could try using a two-dimensional diagram of a cross-section, accompanied by a three-dimensional solid shape.

○ Utilise Moziblox™, a three-dimensional mosaic puzzle, to develop thinking skills — including observation, matching, organising, conceptualising, calculating and planning.

Apart from the tactics suggested above, the success of mathematics relies heavily on the student having a good teacher who uses multisensory modes of teaching, providing plenty of opportunities to practise, and who relates problems to real-world events.

* * *

The advice provided in this chapter is applicable to all subjects, despite focusing on those which students with DCD find particularly demanding. It is usual for secondary-school students to study between nine and thirteen subjects which are intended to provide a broad and balanced education. However, as many subjects require much effort for students with DCD, it may be worth considering allowing these students to take fewer subjects in order to help them to obtain higher grades — maintaining, of course, the core subjects of English, mathematics and science. This should help the student to be more focused and provide more time for them to plan, organise and process information. It may increase the possibility of academic success.

I find it really difficult doing so many subjects at GCSE, because of all the homework, especially the essay writing. I am generally interested in subjects that include less essay writing such as chemistry, physics and maths, and find homework for these subjects much easier to do because it interests me more.

Chapter 6
Pastoral care

Puberty and personal hygiene

Young people attending secondary school are under great pressure to conform and no aspect of this is more important than appearance. Puberty is problematic in itself as racing hormones reap havoc with emotions and appearance. The rapid growth of teenage boys during puberty causes distortions in their body schema. They may be unable to keep up with the staggered changes in growth, and this results in clumsiness. This is true to some extent of all teenagers. However, for those who also have DCD, the challenges are doubled.

Puberty hails the onset of changes in the sweat glands, skin, emotions, body parts, bodily odours, voices and mood. These are not always easy to manage and are felt acutely by students who have DCD. Boys in particular may struggle with aspects of personal hygiene, and they may have less awareness of their body odours than other young people do. In addition co-ordination issues may affect self-care skills. Consequently they may become a prime target of bullying from non-sympathetic, emotionally turbulent peers.

Teasing and manipulation by the opposite sex may leave a young person with DCD questioning their sexuality. Their difficulties with subtlety may lead to an overt interest in sex. Once again this can lead to ridicule and offence. Teachers, with the support and agreement of the students' parents or carers, will need to be very open and honest in their discussions regarding this matter, and supportive of the students' perceived concerns.

Girls with DCD have to manage menstruation. Periods and body odour combine to make these vulnerable girls feel even more repellent to their peers at a time when they need most to feel accepted. Many girls say that they become even clumsier before their period, adding to their struggles to be accepted. There have been some instances of girls with periods who have been teased due to their body odours becoming overconcerned about washing themselves. That may be the first stage of worrying rituals that border on obsessive compulsive disorder. Such behaviour may be a perverse kind of control over a body that has suddenly started to do strange, unpredictable things.

At a late stage puberty brings a new dilemma for boys, who need to start shaving. Many struggle to apply the pressure needed to smooth the razor over the skin. They may require the help of others in performing this routine task well into adulthood. This is not only a concern for boys. Girls wishing to shave their legs have similar difficulties as poor proprioception and co-ordination make shaving a dangerous procedure.

Toothpaste dispenser
www.push-paste.com

Although assistance with puberty and personal hygiene are not part of the remit of a secondary-school teacher, this does have to be taken into account. It is obvious that young people who feel confused about their appearance, relationships and skills, will also feel incompetent in many aspects of school work. It is therefore important that pastoral advice is available which can help with some of the specific issues faced by youngsters with DCD. The **Hygiene hints** list (on page 56) may be given to students who are perhaps facing some of these personal issues.

Dressing and undressing

The importance of wearing a uniform is emphasised at secondary level. Although this is accepted practice, the sensory and motor differences of students with DCD can make this an uncomfortable and anxiety-provoking experience.

One mother recently reported as follows:

> My son was made to stand at the front of the class today, because he could not put his tie on correctly. He usually loosens the neck of the tie to remove it in PE as he cannot co-ordinate the movements to fasten it independently. One of his peers had tightened the knot 'for fun' and he could not slide it up again. The teacher in the following lesson asked him to fasten his tie properly and did not accept that he could not do this, and therefore asked him to stand at the side of the classroom as a humiliating punishment.

> I take quite a while to get changed, things like putting tights on, doing up buttons and tying ties takes me a long time, much to the grievance of my patient friends who have to wait for me after PE.

The main pressure on these students is the need to dress and undress quickly before and after PE lessons. One solution is adaptation of the school uniform. Provided that departure from the uniform rules is agreed in advance, a hand-out such as that shown opposite may be given to parents and carers so that subtle clothing adaptations can be applied. With these adaptations, the student should be able to undress quickly. On the day of a PE lesson, a sports T-shirt may be worn under the school shirt, making the dressing and undressing process quicker and less stressful.

Spring laces
www.ecrater.co.uk

Sensory experiences may also have an impact on the wearing of uniform. Tactile sensations differ in students with DCD, causing certain materials to feel uncomfortable. Particularly irritating are fabric seams, woollen jumpers, labels and ties. The final section of the **Dressing adaptations** sheet for parents and carers has recommendations that should assist with these concerns.

Make-up

DCD is more prevalent in boys, but girls with DCD encounter issues unique to their gender. A major concern is applying make-up. The accurate application of eyeliner, mascara and lipstick requires accurate hand–eye co-ordination, perfect pressure and a very steady hand. The list of **Tips for applying make-up** (on page 56) may be useful.

Dressing adaptations

Tie

Have a tie which has an elastic collar for days when there is sport or PE at school. Alternatively teach your son/daughter how to loosen (but not untie) their tie and remove it over their head.

Shirt

Adapt school shirts by carefully removing all the front buttons. Sew these on top of the button holes. Take circles of soft Velcro and sew these under the buttonhole, place a matching circle of hooked Velcro on the site of each removed button. The shirt can be fastened and unfastened easily without looking obviously different.

At the cuffs, remove the button and reapply using a stalk of elastic, making the cuffs flexible.

Trousers

Replace the upper fastening of trousers with Velcro, then take a thin boot or shoe lace of a colour that matches the trousers. Thread the lace through the zip head and tie a knot. It is far easier to grab a long lace than to pinch a zipper top.

Shoes

Use spring laces, which turn lace-up shoes into slip-ons.

Comfort

If your son/daughter is tactile sensitive, remove labels from the neck of clothing. Run iron-on material tape along rough seams so that the skin is not irritated.

Deep pressure is likely to be more acceptable than a light touch. If needed, provide your son/daughter with a tight vest as this may calm a sensitive sensory system.

Self-care tips

Hygiene hints

Carry wet-wipes so that bottom wiping is thorough.

Change clothes regularly.

Shower daily.

Keep hair in an easy-to-manage style.

Carry sanitising gel.

Seek help early if spots are an issue.

Use an electric toothbrush to guarantee oral hygiene.

Obtain a wall-mounted toothpaste dispenser to use at home or at school. This avoids fiddling with small tops as it is operated by a simple lever or push button.

Enlarge the handle of a toothbrush or razor, using Plastazote tubing to increase your grip.

For girls: use depilatory creams rather that a razor to shave your legs and under-arm hair.

For boys: place a stool in the bathroom so you can shave in a sitting position, stabilising your elbows on the side of the washbasin.

> When I have tried shaving myself, it ends up all uneven because I can't co-ordinate the razor properly. I end up cut to ribbons!

Tips for applying make-up

- *When applying mascara, eyeliner or shadow, sit at a table and stabilise your elbow on the table.*

- *Place wrist weights round the wrist or forearm. These work through the forearm to slow down the movements and help your control.*

- *Alternatively, apply writing weights to the shaft of the mascara or eye liner.*

- *Add Plastazote tubing to your mascara brush handle to improve your grip.*

> I don't wear make-up. I used to put on eye make-up occasionally, but I found it too difficult to apply and take off without help, so I stopped. It's too much trouble, unless it's a special occasion like a wedding.

Friendships

Lack of social awareness may restrict the development of healthy relationships, which in turn will have a bearing on confidence and self-esteem.

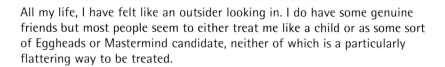

All my life, I have felt like an outsider looking in. I do have some genuine friends but most people seem to either treat me like a child or as some sort of Eggheads or Mastermind candidate, neither of which is a particularly flattering way to be treated.

Boys with DCD are often the butt of jokes and will frequently be teased mercilessly owing to their clumsiness and motor differences. As a consequence they may experience frustration and anger, which can be difficult to manage. Exasperated temper outbursts tend to leave the individual exhausted and drained, leading them to cry or dislocate themselves from their situation. At this age boys are easily influenced by peers, and boys with DCD are liable to be manipulated into participating in situations in which they cannot foresee the outcome. They are especially vulnerable to being manipulated by girls, who may reject them as quickly as they befriend them. This is likely to lead to great frustration and hurt as they struggle to understand the rationale for this behaviour. At this age many young people are exploring their sexuality and instances of manipulation and rejection by girls may cause young boys with DCD to question their gender and sexuality. In conversations about sexual issues they may be less subtle or private than their peers. This can cause hilarity, which is further reinforced by perceived unpopularity.

The majority of students with DCD will have problems with personal space – understanding how close or far to stand or sit in relation to others. They may invade others' personal space unintentionally, sometimes leading to aggressive rebuffs or unfair and cruel sexually related name-calling.

Girls with DCD have to face similar issues. However, more leeway is given for boys to be unsubtle about intimate or potentially private conversations. There is less tolerance of outspoken girls, so conversations which are, for instance, inappropriately loud and perhaps in an inappropriate context may result in ostracisation and gossip.

Teachers may adopt the following strategies to help:

- ❍ Encourage the student to keep busy, joining as many lunchtime clubs as possible so that their time is used constructively and there is less time for them to feel alone and vulnerable.

- ❍ We all have talents and abilities. Try to identify those of the student with DCD and offer support in helping them to excel. Examples include using the computer, playing an instrument, and joining in chess and judo.

- ❍ Encourage the student to go to the library if they find themselves alone in breaks. They will often find there others who are feeling exactly the same and will realise they are less isolated than they thought.

The Socially Speaking Game
by Alison Schroeder
www.ldalearning.com

I always feel so awkward around people, clueless about what to say, how to respond, hardly getting jokes! I feel like such a freak in school, no one really connects with me. I see everyone else really having a connection, and then there's me. Just sat there all on my own. Is this normal?

- ◗ Remind them that adolescence brings changes to all teenagers and that they are not alone in their concerns about appearance, relationships, and so on.

- ◗ If possible provide a forum for developing social skills in which students with similar difficulties can practise social conversations through games, drama and role play. These could include *The Socially Speaking Game*, which aims to build confidence in conversations and behaviour.

- ◗ Teenagers are prone to negative thoughts and feelings. Counterbalance these by asking questions that will help them to put their emotions into perspective. For example: 'Why do you think they said that? What did they gain from saying that? Was it helpful to them? Was it helpful to you? What sort of reaction could you have made?' In this way you can help build resilience and provide coping strategies.

- ◗ Encourage positive thinking and self-talk. Try to encourage each student to think of something they can do. It is easier to believe in negative comments when life is a struggle, and these students need to focus on their abilities and strengths.

Chapter 7
Post–16 and vocational planning

Career planning

Identifying the right career is problematic for many teenagers. It seems that students are being urged to make a decision earlier and earlier, which adds to the difficulty. Those with DCD have the same opportunities as their peers but may need more guidance to prepare them for further/higher education or the workplace. They should certainly not be discouraged from exploring careers in which they are interested – perhaps even passionate about – and should not be deterred by suggestions that they would not succeed because of their difficulties. Determination is the key, and this should be embraced.

Online quiz:
http://www.thewhocarestrust.org.uk/pages/what-job-would-suit-me.html

Careers helpline for young people
www.gov.uk/careers-helpline-for-teenagers

It is important to encourage students to liaise with the school's career adviser to explore individual abilities, interests and aspirations. Most secondary schools recommend a week of work experience in Years 10 and 11. For the student with DCD it is advisable to incorporate further opportunities, even if these have to be arranged during the school holidays. This will allow the student, their work experience supervisor and any potential employer to determine the likely personal and employment adjustments that would need to be put into place prior to a student with DCD being accepted for a position or career in that area. Students may not be aware of the skills they require unless they have real-life experience to help ground their perceptions.

The following strategies will help to guide the student:

- Suggest they make a list of their strengths and weaknesses and discuss these with the school's career adviser.

- Encourage them to complete a career choice questionnaire to identify a range of careers that match their temperament, skills and interests. The careers adviser will have access to these. Discussing their questionnaire results with the careers adviser will help them to identify the field and/or type of job that fits their strengths and weaknesses. Note that the National Careers Helpline also offers help with this decision.

- Tell the student about online advice that they can access themselves.

- Discuss the possibility of turning a hobby into a job. Examples include IT, software development, photography and drama.

- Help the student to plan how to gain first-hand experience of identified occupations, including contacting local employers to identify work-experience opportunities.

● Encourage the student to experience occupations that interest them on a voluntary/holiday basis if possible.

● Advise the student to be realistic. Take into account their predicted grades and decide on the subjects for which they are likely to get the best results.

● If the student's career choice requires them to complete a degree or other qualification, tell them how to investigate the support services available to them at the relevant institutions of higher and further education. One that strives to be inclusive will have a student-support network which will include writing support, equipment assessment and provision, flexible assessment methods, curriculum adaptations and material differentiation. Many of these services are grouped under a collective term such as 'Disability advice' or 'Disability support'. This may seem somewhat exclusive and stigmatising, but the support offered should be completely confidential and would be provided on an as-needed basis.

The services likely to be available at institutions of higher and further education are shown opposite, **Reasonable accommodations for students with DCD**. This should be given to students to help them as they make the transition from school to higher or further education.

When applying for a job or a university/college place, whether a student discloses their difficulties or not is a decision that is personal to them. If they decide to do so, advise them to try to describe them positively, emphasising what they can do and the strategies that have been implemented to help.

Be aware that in both education and employment there is funding available to make adjustments. The employer or education provider may not always be aware of this, and the student may decide to inform them.

Work Choice:
www.gov.uk/work-choice

For students with complex needs, such as DCD and autism, an organisation called Work Choice offers help, aiming to support students whose needs cannot be met through other work programmes – such as Access to Work – or through simple workplace adjustments. Work Choice assists students who need more specialised support with finding employment or keeping a job.

Legislation

Students with DCD are supported by legislation pertaining to disability, even though they may not perceive themselves as being disabled. This unfortunate negative term is currently used to support the transition from secondary school to employment and further/higher education. Some employers may argue that DCD is not a disability and therefore refuse to make any concessions or make reasonable adjustments. However the Equality Act, which replaced most of the Disability Discrimination Act (DDA) from October 2010, states that a person has a disability 'if he or she has a physical or mental impairment and the impairment has a substantial and long-term adverse effect on his or her ability to carry out normal day-to-day activities'.

Reasonable accommodations for students with DCD

○ Hand-outs provided prior to lectures. These should be printed on pastel-coloured paper and/or in large print where necessary. This will allow the student to concentrate on listening and understanding the lecture/seminar rather than struggling to take notes.

○ Extra time may be given for the submission of assignments and in examinations.

○ Tape recorders / Dictaphones should be allowed in lectures (providing the material being taught is not of a sensitive nature, and the individual lecturer agrees).

○ Help will be given with the structure and organisation of assignments.

○ Many institutions of higher education accept only word-processed submissions. Assignments are usually submitted electronically. This negates any worries about handwriting legibility in circumstances other than examinations. Guidance will be given about the procedure.

○ Depending on the outcome of an assessment, a scribe or note-taker may be allocated to write notes in lectures on the student's behalf.

○ A laptop and appropriate software may be provided. Suitable products include Texthelp (for grammar, spelling, etc.), Inspiration (for mind mapping) and Livescribe (for note-taking).

○ Students may be allowed to take exams in a separate room to avoid distractions.

○ Each student will have a personal tutor who will be an advocate for their needs while in higher education. They will support the student throughout their studies and ensure that reasonable accommodations identified by the student support service are in place.

The guidance for the Equality Act, written by the Office for Disability (2010), provides an example of impairment using a young man with DCD:

A young man who has dyspraxia (DCD) experiences a range of effects which include difficulty co-ordinating physical movements. He is frequently knocking over cups and bottles of drink and cannot combine two activities at the same time, such as walking while holding a plate of food upright, without spilling the food.

This has a substantial adverse effect on his ability to carry out normal day-to-day activities such as making a drink and eating.

DSAs
www.gov.uk/disabled-students-allowances-dsas

The DDA says that employers and education providers are not allowed to discriminate against the student or treat them less favourably because of their impairment (e.g. not employing them or admitting them to a course just because of their organisational and motor difficulties). They are required by law to make reasonable adjustments to enable the individual to do a course or job – for example, by providing specialist equipment or software.

In order for an education provider or employer to make reasonable adjustments, they need to have a good understanding of DCD – and other conditions – in the first place. Financial constraints may be limiting; however under the Equalities Act 2010 financial resources have been allocated to support students. Information on Disabled Students' Allowances (DSAs) is available online.

Difficulties learning to drive

Many post-16 employment opportunities may specify driving as a pre-requisite skill. This can be problematic for students with DCD who are 17 or above as visual–spatial difficulties may have an impact on the judgement of speed and space so necessary for safe driving.

Driving Tips
www.downloads.life-in-motion.co.uk

There is evidence that young adults with DCD make twice as many steering adjustments when driving down a straight course and negotiating a bend than their peers do. Also, they are more reluctant to decelerate on time before going round a bend. They may be slower to react to hazards. For example, in deOliveira and Wann's (2011) research, a sample of young people with DCD took 50 per cent more time to react to pedestrians who walked towards their path than other drivers did. The research also showed that auditory distractions had a detrimental effect on reactions to hazards. All this may be pushing young adults with DCD beyond driving safety thresholds.

Despite these concerns, it is possible for these students to master this complex skill. Most students consider learning to drive in school Year 12, when they turn 17 and can obtain a provisional licence. It is worth considering helping students with DCD to prepare in advance for the theory test, at the age of 15 to 16, so that they have the opportunity of overlearning selected skills.

You could consider setting up a pre-driving preparation club as a school-based activity, both for students with DCD and those with developmental differences affecting co-ordination, attention and perception. The **Tips for driving** sheet, opposite, may be useful.

Tips for driving

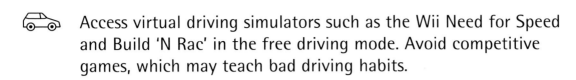 Access virtual driving simulators such as the Wii Need for Speed and Build 'N Rac' in the free driving mode. Avoid competitive games, which may teach bad driving habits.

 Use virtual games to help you learn to respond quickly to unexpected obstacles.

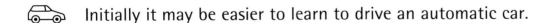 Learn the Highway Code and use a variety of methods to test and check your knowledge. There are some excellent apps for iPhones, iPod Touch and iPads such as these:
- ○ Hazard Perception Test
- ○ iTheory Driving Test UK
- ○ BSM Theory Test
- ○ Theory Test for UK Car Drivers
- ○ UK Driving Genius Lite.

Use online quizzes to test your Highway Code knowledge.

If possible, start learning to drive off-road in order to become familiar with handling a car independently of driving on a road. It is possible to do this from the age of 14 years. For information about one provider see www.driveat15.com

Seek out a sympathetic and understanding instructor when you start to learn on the road. Provide them with the practical tips to help you from Life in Motion Ltd:

www.downloads.life-in-motion.co.uk

Initially it may be easier to learn to drive an automatic car.

References

Addy, L.M. (2004) *Speed-Up! A Kinaesthetic Programme to Develop Fluent Handwriting*. Cambridge: LDA.

Barnett, A., S. Henderson, B. Scheib and J. Schulz (2007) *Detailed Assessment of Speed of Handwriting*. Oxford: Harcourt Assessment.

Davies, P.L., and W.J. Gavin (2007) 'Validating the diagnosis of sensory processing disorders with EEG technology'. *American Journal of Occupational Therapy* 61, 176–189.

deOliveira, R.F., and J.P. Wann (2011) 'Driving skills of young adults with developmental coordination disorder: regulating speed and coping with distraction'. *Research in Developmental Disabilities* 32(4), 1301–8

Foulder-Hughes, L.A., and R.W. Cooke (2003) 'Motor, cognitive, and behavioural disorders in children born very preterm'. *Developmental Medicine and Child Neurology* 45(2), 97–103.

Kirby, A., D. Sugden, S. Beveridge and L. Edwards (2008) 'Developmental coordination (DCD) in adults and adolescents'. *Journal of Research in Special Educational Needs* 8, 120–131.

Lingam, R., L Hunt, J. Golding, M. Jongmans and A. Emond (2009) 'Prevalence of DCD using the DSM-IV at 7 years of age: a UK population-based study'. *Paediatrics* 123(4), 693700.

Marlow, N., D. Wolke, M.A. Bracewell and members of the EICure study group (2005) 'Neurologic and developmental disability at six years of age after extremely preterm birth'. *New England Journal of Medicine* 6. 352(1), 9–19.

Piek, J.P., M.J. Dyck, A. Nieman, M. Anderson, D. Hay and L.M. Smith (2004) 'The relationship between motor co-ordination, executive functioning and attention in school aged children'. *Archives of Clinical Neuropsychology* 19, 1063–1076.

Querne, L, P. Berquin, M. Vernier-Hauvette, S. Fall, L. Deltour and M. Meyer (2008) 'Dysfunction of the attentional brain network in children with developmental coordination disorder (DCD): a fMRI study'. *Brain Research* 1244, 89–102.

Wilson, B.N., S.G. Crawford, D. Green, A. Aylott and B.J. Kaplan (2009) 'Psychometric properties of the Revised Developmental Co-ordination Disorder Questionnaire'. *Physical and Occupational Therapy in Pediatrics* 29(2), 182–202.